Regional Impacts of Federal Fiscal Policy

Regional Impacts of Federal Fiscal Policy

Theory and Estimation of Economic Incidence

Thanos Catsambas
Yale University

Lexington Books
D.C. Heath and Company
Lexington, Massachusetts
Toronto

044269

Library of Congress Cataloging in Publication Data

Catsambas, Thanos.
  Regional impacts of Federal fiscal policy.

  Bibliography: p.
  Includes index.
  1. Tax incidence—United States. 2. United States—Appropriations and expenditures. 3. Fiscal policy—United States. I. Title.
HJ2322.A3C37   336'.02'73   77-12282
ISBN 0-669-01953-4

*HJ
2322
.A3C37
1978*

International Standard Book Number: 0-669-01953-4

Library of Congress Catalog Card Number: 77-12282

To Lena, thanks to whom,
and to Marika and Titika, despite whom,
this book is a reality.

Contents

List of Figures

List of Tables

Acknowledgments

This book has evolved from my doctoral research at Yale. I wish to express my appreciation to Professors Guy Orcutt, Richard Ruggles, and John Quigley, who channeled my work into a fruitful and organized investigation.

I am particularly indebted to Professor Quigley who read the entire manuscript and offered several constructive suggestions during the transformation of my research into this book. For any remaining sins of omission or commission, I claim sole responsibility.

Apart from his valuable guidance, Professor Ruggles, an old-time friend at Yale, also provided the basic financial support through a National Science Foundation grant to the National Bureau of Economic Research. I thank him wholeheartedly.

Mr. John Woodford of the Yale Computer Center was very helpful during the empirical implementation of this study. It is fair to emphasize that most of our conversations began as academic queries, regardless of how they usually ended.

Since I was out of the country, while writing a good part of the book, I would like to thank three persons for their kind assistance while I was away: Mr. James Trask, who promptly processed numerous computer programs for me under some particularly tight time constraints; his help is gratefully acknowledged. Dr. Nick Bacopoulos, who contributed several good ideas dealing with small and big problems. And Mrs. Jean Gemmell, whose efficient and excellent typing enabled me to meet a number of important deadlines.

This book owes its existence to my partner-in-life, Lena Valavani.

Athens, Greece   *Thanos Catsambas*
January 1978

Regional Impacts of
Federal Fiscal Policy

1

The Concept of Fiscal Incidence: History and Present Methodology

Introduction

The most popular quantitative exercise in public finance has been the estimation of tax incidence and the distribution of tax burdens. For decades, economists have sought to answer the perennial question, "Who bears the tax burden?" Numerous studies have dealt with some variation of the central theme. Until recently, very few of these studies had included estimates of the distribution of benefits from government services. But in the past few years, it has become increasingly apparent that a one-sided view of the public sector could only lead to an incomplete and perhaps misleading evaluation of government activities. Most current contributions to the subject, therefore, focus on the concept of *net* fiscal incidence, which requires a systematic analysis of both taxation and public expenditures.

The concept and theories of fiscal incidence have long been esoteric to the layman, but even among economists their importance is not always fully appreciated. The reason for this is that the implications of incidence are taken for granted too often and by too many people. The tax and expenditure variables used in many theoretical models (other than those that address themselves to *ad hoc* incidence questions) are implicitly assumed to reflect the final impact of a given policy action. But to the fiscal economist, the link between fiscal policy and final effect is not always self-explanatory. The distinction between statutory liability and ultimate incidence holds a central position in the theory and applications of public finance. If we do not know which individuals are *ultimately* affected by a government measure, we cannot explain how a particular fiscal action may influence the behavior of households, firms, markets, and indeed, the whole economy.

In the area of income distribution the concept of incidence is an indispensable prerequisite for any kind of investigation. Their linkage is so intimate that, in a sense, the terms "income redistribution" and "fiscal incidence" may be regarded as equivalent. The equivalence basically holds because incidence is a direct result of a fiscal action, even in the absence of conscious redistributional policies.

It thus becomes evident that public sector activity, regardless of its specific objectives, rests on weak foundations unless its actual effects are known and understood. This statement assumes even greater significance in the light of recent concerted efforts to improve the measurement of national economic performance and to establish a more disaggregated framework for the evaluation of government interference. In particular, it is becoming increasingly apparent that conventional aggregative indices provide an inadequate summary of economic performance. The advantages and disadvantages of different types of public policy must be considered in terms of their effects upon households on the basis not only of economic but also of social indicators, such as age, sex, family size, and other demographic or regional characteristics.

Within the framework of a systematic analysis of the impact of the public sector on households and firms, the spatial disaggregation of government taxes and expenditures is central to an evaluation of particular fiscal policy patterns. So long as regional estimates of taxes and expenditures are consistent with macroeconomic accounts, they provide an essential infrastructure for the analysis of interactions between groups of firms or households and various levels of government. Needless to emphasize, for such estimates to be useful from an analytical viewpoint, they must reflect the "true" incidence of receipts and outlays. The extent to which this can be meaningfully accomplished is itself a topic of some research importance.

Subject of Study

The purpose of this study is to provide estimates of federal burdens and benefits, by state, for the United States for the calendar year 1972, and to examine their implications. Although the growing importance of the state and local sectors should not be overlooked, the activity of the central government is still the most vital function of the public sector, if only because federal policies frequently aim at specific economic or social objectives, which carry many redistributional ramifications. Thus, the net fiscal incidence of the central government may greatly redistribute resources spatially, widening or narrowing the disparities caused by comparative advantage or by conscious regional development policies.

In 1972 the revenues and outlays of the federal government were as summarized in table 1-1.

As far as taxes are concerned, the taxonomy used in this study parallels that of table 1-1, except for selective sales taxes and customs duties, which are discussed at a greater degree of detail. With respect to expenditures, our analysis involves both a more disaggregated taxonomy and a different functional classification. Total distributed burdens amount to 91 percent of federal revenues, and total distributed benefits to 97 percent of federal outlays.

Before we turn to the examination of individual taxes and expenditures, we discuss the most important methodological aspects of incidence, which is the underlying link in the various parts of this study. This is done in the remainder

Table 1-1
Summary of Federal Taxes and Expenditures, 1972
(in billions of dollars)

Taxes			Expenditures		
		Percent of total revenues			*Percent of total outlays*
Personal Income	$93.354	40	Health, Labor, Welfare	$87.714	36
Payroll	62.467	27			
Corporate Income	32.166	14	Defense, Space and International Affairs	85.872	35
Selective Sales	16.847	7			
Estate and Gift	5.436	2	General Government	24.469	10
Customs Duties	3.283	1	Veterans' Benefits and Services	12.626	5
Other[a]	19.682	9	Commerce, Transportation, and Housing	11.202	4.5
Total	$233.235	100%			
			Agriculture and Natural Resources	9.215	4
			Education	6.517	2.5
			Other[b]	7.587	3
			Total	$245.202	100%

Sources: *Survey of Current Business* (U.S. Department of Commerce, Office of Business Economics, July 1974); and the *Annual Report of the Commissioner of the Internal Revenue Service* (U.S. Department of the Treasury, Internal Revenue Service, 1972 and 1973).
[a]Includes miscellaneous general revenue, current charges and "other taxes." These have been omitted from the present study.
[b]Includes general revenue sharing, postal services and some minor items in transportation and public utilities. These have been omitted from the present study.

of this chapter. The next section provides a historical introduction to the notion of fiscal incidence in conjunction with the most significant contributions to the subject. The following section concentrates on previous studies that have examined the same general question as the present investigation, namely that of geographical incidence. Finally, the last part of this chapter presents a careful analysis of the definitional aspects of incidence that are crucial for the purposes of this monograph.

A Historical Overview of the Theory and Measurement of Fiscal Incidence

Although the underlying theoretical propositions on which studies of fiscal incidence are based can in principle be applied to a great variety of distributions, the overwhelming majority of papers in this area have attempted to provide an allocation of taxes or expenditures (or both) by income classes. Distributions by family size are sometimes made; other types of distribution, such as by occupation or by geographical region, are indeed rare.

In the area of taxation, the earliest detailed study on the distribution of taxes in the United States was that by Mabel Newcomer in the Twentieth Century Fund research project of 1937.[1] Carl Shoup, however, reports[2] an even earlier study prepared by the Colwyn Commission in the United Kingdom in 1927. But that study covered only the taxes of the central government, whereas the Newcomer study was apparently the first in any country to include taxes of all levels of government. An interesting feature of both studies is the employment of the so-called "typical-family technique": This methodology uses the tax law, but no tax collection data. Given a family's consumption and income levels and patterns, and with the aid of certain other appropriate assumptions, the tax rates can be applied to yield a tax bill for that family. The procedure is repeated for similarly specified families at other income levels.

The "typical-family" technique gave place to the "total-tax-bill" technique as early as 1941, and the latter has since then been almost exclusively utilized in the distribution of tax burdens. This methodology uses tax collection data and does not require information on tax rates, tax bases, or other similar notions. The allocation of taxes is achieved by making use of a set of incidence assumptions, some of which are usually alternative propositions about the shifting and incidence of a given tax.

The first study of this type, entitled *Who Pays the Taxes?*, was written by Helen Tarasov, under the supervision of Gerhard Colm,[3] and was soon followed by various similar contributions whose number kept growing during the 1950s and the 1960s. Of the numerous studies in this area two deserve special mention: the first is a study by Musgrave et al., which appeared in 1951 and soon became the object of an extensive controversy about its empirical results.[4] Its most startling finding was that 28.1 percent of the income of those in the under $1,000 class was being taken in taxation, compared with 29.2 percent for all income groups together. The arguments took the form of a series of comments, rebuttals, and rejoinders between Musgrave and Frane on the one hand, and Haskell Walk, Gerhard Colm, and Rufus S. Tucker on the other.[5] As Shoup observes, "Anyone who wants to become acquainted with the chief conceptual and computational pitfalls in this area will benefit from a study of this sheaf of excellent analyses."[6]

The second study that deserves special mention appeared in 1974: *Who*

Bears the Tax Burden?, by J.A. Pechman and B.A. Okner.[7] The analysis by Pechman and Okner, which relates to the year 1966, broke new ground by computing the tax burden on the basis of a microunit data file for a representative sample of 72,000 families, which has become known as the MERGE file.[8] Although this study is fundamentally based on the same "total-tax-bill" technique, the extensive use of computer methodology has enabled the authors to present estimates not only for family units, but also for several significant demographic and economic subgroups. Furthermore, they presented estimates on the basis of eight different sets of tax incidence assumptions. Their major finding was that the U.S. tax system is essentially proportional for the vast majority of families.

In 1951, John H. Adler presented a tax distribution for 1946-1947, together with a distribution of the benefits of government services and transfer payments for that year.[9] He concluded that the fiscal system as a whole was progressive for both of those years. In the period that followed Adler's study, estimates of the distribution of benefits from public expenditures were rarely included in studies of fiscal incidence, and if so, they were so rough as to be rather uninteresting. It was not until 1964 that a very thoughtful contribution to the theory and empirical estimation of net fiscal incidence appeared in the series of studies prepared for the Canadian Royal Commission on Taxation. This monograph, entitled *The Incidence of Taxes and Public Expenditures in the Canadian Economy*, was written by W. Irwin Gillespie, who made a careful effort to set up a clear framework and to point out the major difficulties and limitations of his work.[10] Apart from the specifics of his study, Gillespie should primarily be given credit for his pioneering determination to place due emphasis on the expenditure side of government and to treat taxation and public expenditures on an equal footing. His subsequent study on public expenditures in the U.S. economy is perhaps the most extensively quoted work on the subject, even though it has not gone unchallenged.[11]

Of the most recent studies in the area of net fiscal incidence, the work of David A. Dodge on the Canadian economy, and of R. Musgrave et al. on the U.S. economy should be mentioned. The former, a well-documented and methodologically detailed study, provides empirical estimates of fiscal incidence for 1970, along with simulation results of the differential incidence for the same year under a set of policy changes, which actually occurred later in the Canadian economy. The latter updates to 1968 levels earlier estimates of net fiscal incidence by income class, and draws on the MERGE file (mentioned earlier), although its degree of utilization is left unclear by the authors.[12]

This brief introduction to the history of fiscal incidence investigations of the American economy was centered around studies of incidence by income classes, if only because it is within the great number of such studies that the pioneering works and benchmark contributions are to be found. We next turn to a more detailed review of the works that are akin to our study, namely the investigations of geographical incidence.

A Brief Review of Previous Investigations
of Geographical Incidence

In the area of geographical incidence there exists only one study that has attempted to provide concurrent estimates of federal revenues and expenditures for states and regions for the fiscal years 1965-1967. This is a report prepared by the Legislative Reference Service of the Library of Congress, (henceforth referred to as "The Congressional Study") and until now it has served as the only guide to the spatial distribution of public sector activity.[13] The other works in this area have dealt exclusively either with the revenue or with the expenditure side alone. The best known of these are the studies by Mushkin on both taxes and expenditures,[14] and the series on the allocations of federal taxes among states (and more recently among metropolitan areas), which is published by the Tax Foundation on a more or less routine basis.[15] Besides the works just mentioned, every other paper in this area has been limited in scope, either in terms of its specific topic (such as an analysis of a single tax or expenditure), or in terms of its geographical coverage (analysis for only a particular region).

Geographical Incidence of Federal Taxes

The *personal income tax* has always been the easiest to deal with. All of these studies accept the widely held assumption that the statutory and economic incidence of the tax coincide, and then proceed to allocate its geographical burden by specific distributional procedures whose quality has improved over the years.

Payroll taxes have been treated identically with respect to the incidence assumption. It has been accepted that half of the burden falls on consumers in terms of higher prices, and half is borne by employees. The most interesting feature of the studies mentioned earlier is precisely the ready acceptance and use of the fifty-fifty formula for the incidence of this tax. It is not so much the assumption *per se,* as it is the employed percentages. But if there is uncertainty about the incidence of the payroll tax, any combination of shifting is as arbitrary a hypothesis as any other. It therefore would have been more appropriate to use the two extreme forms of the assumption, namely no shifting and 100 percent forward shifting, and thus determine the sensitivity of the final estimate.[a]

---

[a]It is also noteworthy that none of the studies has justified its use of the "fifty-fifty" formula on the statutory incidence of the payroll tax, which is half on the employer and

There is also little controversy over the incidence of *estate and gift taxes,* which are assumed to fall directly on the donor or decedent.

The well-known controversy over the incidence of the *corporate income tax* is reflected (although not exhaustively) in all of the studies that have calculated geographical tax burdens. There is no consensus about the direction and degree of the shifting: Selma Mushkin believes that the burden falls exclusively on shareholders, while the Congressional Study takes the view that this is true for only half of it, and that the other half is shifted forward to consumers. The views held by the Tax Foundation have not apparently reached a steady-state. In the earlier years, the uncertainty was thought to be so great that the total burden was very roughly allocated on the basis of personal income. In the reports of 1957 and 1964 it was assumed that half of the burden is borne by stockholders and half by consumers. Finally, in the report of 1974, the view about consumers was retained, but the other half was extended to property owners in general. The latter study recognizes the widely divergent opinions in this area, but concludes that, by following the foregoing procedure, it "adopts a middleground." This is, of course, a very surprising conclusion, especially since the labeling is not explained any further. Otherwise, the assumption adopted by both the Tax Foundation and the Congressional Study suffers from the same drawback mentioned earlier in connection with the payroll tax, namely that the choice of a specific percentage in dividing the shifting mechanism is arbitrary.

The weakest aspect of every previous study has unquestionably been their treatment of *excise taxes.* Since this category includes selective sales taxes and duties on a wide variety of specific commodities, it is possible that the burden of such levies is shifted differentially. The single most important oversight has been the failure to distinguish between commodities used in final consumption and those used as intermediate goods. For even with the assumption of complete forward shifting, the burden of taxes imposed on intermediate goods will necessarily fall on a wider group of consumers than those in direct final consumption.

Geographical Incidence of Federal Expenditures

If the estimation of tax burdens derives from an extensive body of economic theory, but the results are uncertain because of many controversial issues and the lack of satisfactory data, no comparable theoretical framework supports expenditure allocations. In the case of fiscal benefits the problems are thus not only empirical but also conceptual. The complications arising in the geographical

---

half on the employee. Even if that had been the case, however, the underlying reasoning could have hardly been considered as rigorous. Once a decision to shift a tax is made by a concerned party (for example, the employer), it is impossible to determine *a priori* the intended extent—let alone the actual outcome—after all the interacting market forces have played their part.

distribution of public expenditure benefits have therefore been a restraining factor for systematic research in this area. The Tax Foundation, which has presented estimates of the distribution of benefits by income class, has not as yet attempted such a distribution in the spatial dimension. Hence, there have been only two attempts to tackle this problem in a more or less complete fashion—the 1957 paper by Mushkin, and the second part of the 1968 Congressional Study.

The Mushkin paper is an expository article on the many intricate facets of the geographical distribution of federal expenditures. Although the author does provide two sets of estimates (based on two different concepts), her purpose is clearly to present a careful analysis of the various methodological alternatives and their relation to the underlying theoretical foundations. The latter objective is not analyzed sufficiently, but Mushkin succeeds in presenting a systematic investigation of the relevant concepts, methods, assumptions, and procedures. Her discussion centers around a well-explained introduction to the "dollar-flow" and the "benefit" concepts of public expenditures. "The benefit approach," says Mushkin, "traces federal expenditures to the recipients of the services and payments for which the federal programs are designed. In contrast, a dollar-flow approach is designed to trace the funds from their taxpayer sources to the recipients—federal employees, other individuals, and families receiving welfare payments and benefits, holders of the public debt, and those who produce the goods and services which go into commodities purchased by the federal government."[16]

This is, of course, a valid distinction, and the author provides numerous examples of the diverse methodologies required by the two different concepts. But when it comes to choosing between them, Mushkin pleads indifference. In fact, she professes that "the two measures . . . serve different purposes and are useful for different kinds of analysis."[17] This is a surprising conclusion, especially since she subsequently admits that a dollar-flow measure "would be analogous to federal tax collections . . . on the receipt side of the budget."[18] Yet in her previously mentioned study on tax burdens, the author had clearly recognized the inadequacy of collection data and the need for "incidence" analysis. Why, then, did she not adhere to the same principle for the expenditure side? Most probably the author was forced to accept both concepts as a result of the existing tradeoffs between theoretical validity and empirical applicability. She accepts the "benefit" principle as conceptually correct, but she also accepts the "dollar-flow" principle for reasons of convenience, given the empirical difficulties that beset the former. In general, the Mushkin study had provided enough analytical insight to have served as a point of departure for various research efforts in this broad area. That it did not is rather astonishing.

The Congressional Study, on the other hand, has a clearly empirical orientation. The expenditure allocations are based on the "dollar-flow" concept and are adequately documented, although some implicit assumptions are left unclear. Apart from this methodological choice of the "dollar-flow" concept, the other most important limitation of the Congressional Study lies in the treatment of expenditures only by *type* of transaction. Although this drawback is less serious than it would have been under a "benefit" approach, the suppression of information relating to the *object* of expenditure necessarily obscures, if not the end result, certainly the underlying methods and procedures. It thus appears that, from the analytical point of view, the usefulness of the expenditure allocations of the Congressional Study is rather limited.

In conclusion, considering the rich, if not incontrovertible, literature in the area of tax incidence, and the much fewer, but equally stimulating, works in the area of expenditure incidence (particularly the contributions to the theory of public goods), the number of studies that have dealt with the geographical dimension of incidence is too small to be considered satisfactory. But it is also true that it is very difficult to do justice to such investigations, because their empirical statements are necessarily conditional on many behavioral assumptions.

Fiscal Incidence and Economic Theory: Methodology and Terminology Specification

To quote T.A. Stockfisch, "the concept of 'incidence' means too many things to be of much use to either tax specialists or students of general fiscal economics."[19] Indeed, this definitional ambiguity frequently causes much unnecessary controversy as different investigators discuss different topics under the (mistaken) impression that they treat the same topic. The source of confusion usually lies in the causal-genetic classification of the term, which is required under each of its functional divisions (such as *personal, regional* or *intertemporal* incidence).

Within a general-equilibrium framework, the term "incidence" should be allowed to reflect the myriad of interacting effects that follow the initial withdrawal of purchasing power, in the case of taxation, or injection of purchasing power, in the case of expenditures. As a result of a given fiscal action, a rational economic actor is expected to modify his economic behavior, which in turn may have considerable short- and long-run repercussions on micro- and macroeconomic activity. In the case of the individual income tax, for example, a change in the tax structure could affect the macroeconomy via (1) an effect upon the demand for products, (2) an effect upon savings, and (3) an effect upon labor supply. Alternatively, a change in the corporate income tax could produce (1) an effect upon the supply of the product, (2) an effect upon investment, and (3) an effect upon the demand for labor.

Furthermore, in a general-equilibrium sense, emphasis should also be placed on the dynamic aspects of incidence by considering the trajectories of the economic phenomena in the context of an evolutionary economy. (The introduction of the time dimension, however, does not *per se* constitute an improvement in the analytical power of a given model. A short-run model may conceivably be more useful for policy purposes than a long-run adaptive scheme.)

It thus becomes obvious that, from a general-equilibrium point of view, the cumulative repercussions of fiscal activity extend beyond the customary concepts of "burdens" or "benefits," because any attempt to separate the manifold interactions may render the concept of "incidence" questionable. The psychological reactions to saving, consumption, and investment on the part of economic agents influence the volume and the structure of effective supply and demand, and thus total economic performance.

The problem, of course, is that a general-equilibrium analysis poses insurmountable difficulties, both theoretical and empirical. Perhaps more important than the heroic construction of a general-equilibrium model is the interpretation of its results. As Geoge F. Break has aptly remarked, "the comprehensive, but incomprehensible, general-equilibrium analysis [incorporates] every conceivable effect in its many-equation models of the economy and consequently [generates] results whose significance, or reliability, is almost impossible to determine."[20]

In the face of this quandary, several attempts have been made to restrict the use of the term to special kinds of fiscal effects. Stockfisch, for example, distinguishes five categories: (1) the income effect, (2) the price reallocation effect, (3) the spenders' welfare effect, (4) the incentive effect, and (5) the distributive effect.[21] These are to be compared with Musgrave's three classifications: (1) resource transfer, (2) output effects, and (3) distribution effects.[22]

The temptation of partial analysis is realized through the use of a *ceteris paribus* clause. This is, perhaps, debatable for the purposes of econometric analysis, but it appears reasonable for studies like the present one, whose results do not represent statistical estimates but, rather, a quantitative realization of theoretical deductions. It is also true that for investigations of such a nature the use of a general-equilibrium analysis is impossible because the very structure of markets in the absence of government becomes problematic. David Dodge summarizes this point very eloquently: "It is not possible to account for higher order effects of *all* government activity since the institutional framework of markets would be so different in the total absence of government that none of the estimates of behavioral response to policy changes made in the current institutional setting would be valid."[23]

Yet the use of partial-equilibrium analysis does not *per se* resolve the definitional questions of "incidence." Different authors have given different interpretations to the term and have accordingly handled different problems. The inescapable conclusion seems to be the existence of a trade-off: the broader the scope of a study, the more restrictive its framework; and vice-versa, for sharply focused investigations.

Definition of Incidence in Present Study

In the light of the foregoing discussion, it seems desirable to interpret, for the purpose of the present study, the term "incidence" as a theoretically distinct phenomenon which, though closely related to other fiscal effects, deserves an analytic separation. This immediately poses the complication that particular estimates of revenue and expenditure items may be suspect. Nevertheless, such estimates do provide a reasonable benchmark for the analysis of marginal changes in central government policy, at least as long as they do not reflect controversial assumptions.

Within this framework, the term "incidence" is intimately connected with the concept of "shifting." In the case of taxation, the term "shifting" refers to the economic process, operating through the price mechanism, by which the direct money burden is transferred from the point of its statutory liability to its final "resting" place. Similarly, the term "snatching"[24] refers to the same process in the case of public expenditures. Conceivably, the shifting mechanism may be directed backward (to the factors of production), or forward (to the buyers of the good or service). (In the European literature it has also been found useful to distinguish the so-called "cross-shifting," which refers to the eventuality of shifting the tax not through the charged article but via another one.)

The term "incidence," therefore, should be understood to refer to the location of the ultimate burden or benefit of the tax or the expenditure. This immediately points to the fact that we can distinguish three forms of incidence:

1. The *statutory* incidence, based on the letter of the law.
2. The *intended* or *expected* incidence, based on the spirit of the law.
3. The *actual* or *effective* incidence.

From the analytical point of view it is only the third form that matters.

We may thus proceed to define as "fiscal incidence" *the changes in relative income positions of well-defined economic units of observation, which come about through direct monetary transactions and are due to the fiscal activity of the public sector.*

This definition lends itself to the estimation of geographic fiscal incidence by breaking down total tax burdens and expenditure benefits on the basis of a chosen jurisdiction, such as the state or the county. Yet the concept is still one step short of operational: we need to give an empirical content to the notions of "total tax burdens" and "total expenditure benefits."

Our aim is achieved by equating total burdens to total revenue collected and total benefits to total costs of public expenditures. This is an important assumption, because total burden may exceed total revenue, if proper account is taken of the resulting interference with consumer choice or of the reallocation of resources. Similarly, total benefits may exceed total costs of provision, insofar as individuals place a greater value on public goods than the cost of their provision. It should also be noted that expressing "burdens" (that is, loss of utility) and "benefits" (that is, gains in utility) as dollar amounts implies constant marginal utility of income for all individuals.

The foregoing remarks may be depicted diagrammatically, as in figure 1-1. The impact of the federal government is felt at every one of these stages. A movement from (1) to (4) entails an improvement in the underlying theoretical considerations. In principle, therefore, the last group of this taxomony would be the most appropriate concept to employ, because it involves both the direct and indirect effects. In other words, stage (4) roughly corresponds to a general-equilibrium methodology. But the resulting complications render this stage impracticable.

An operational concept of incidence, which corresponds to the definition presented earlier, is reflected in stage (3). Both stages (1) and (2) use the same control totals as (3), but the difference lies in the fact that the latter incorporates the effort to go beyond statutory incidence and to account for both the tax "shifting" and the benefit "snatching" or "relinquishing." Figure 1-1 clearly delineates the limits for a congruent treatment of the revenue and the expenditure sides, and suggests the degree to which any deviation (intentional or not) from a symmetrical procedure may have bearing on the desirable notion of "*net* fiscal incidence."

Finally, table 1-2 summarizes the incidence assumptions used in this study.

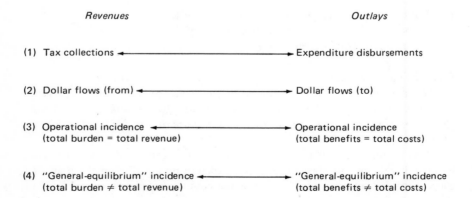

Figure 1-1. Levels of Impact of the Public Sector

Table 1-2
Summary of Tax and Expenditure Incidence Assumptions

		Incidence Assumption	
		Pages	
Taxes		Discussed	Implemented
Personal Income	on initial payers	15-18	27
Payroll	on workers	18-20	27
Estate	"on decedents"	26	28
Gift	on donors	26	28
Corporate Income	i) on consumers		
	ii) on owners of corporate capital		
	iii) on owners of capital at large	20-26	27-28
	iv) on workers	35-38	40-48
Excise	on consumers		
Expenditures			
Private Goods[a]	on initial recipients		63, 67, 68
Transfers	on initial recipients	55-61	62-63
Grants-in-Aid	on residents of relevant state		62-63
Public Goods	i) on recipients of private goods		
	ii) 25 percent on recipients of private goods; 75 percent on all state residents equally	75-84	84-85

[a]Assumptions of individual components are discussed on pp. 63, 67, 68.

Notes

1. M. Newcomer, *Studies in Current Tax Problems*, New York: Twentieth Century Fund, 1937.

2. In *Quantitative Research in Taxation and Government Expenditure,* Fiftieth Anniversary Colloquium IV. New York: National Bureau of Economic Research, 1972.

3. G. Colm and H. Tarasov, *Who Pays the Taxes?* Monograph No. 3, Washington, D.C.: Temporary National Economic Committee, 1941.

4. R.A. Musgrave, J.J. Carroll, L.D. Cook, and L. Frane, "Distribution of Tax Payments by Income Groups: A Case Study for 1948," *National Tax Journal* 4 (March 1951).

5. See *National Tax Journal* 4 (September 1951) and 5 (March 1952).

6. Shoup, *Quantitative Research*, p. 9.

7. Joseph A. Pechman and Benjamin A. Okner, *Who Bears the Tax Burden?*, Studies in Government Finance. Washington, D.C.: The Brookings Institution, 1974

8. The MERGE file was subsequently used by Musgrave et al. for the estimation of benefits from government expenditures as well.

9. "The Fiscal System, the Distribution of Income, and Public Welfare," chapter VIII in Kenyon E. Poole, *Fiscal Policies and the American Economy*, Englewood Cliffs, N.J.: Prentice-Hall, 1951.

10. No. 2 in *Studies of the Royal Commission on Taxation*, Canada, September 1964.

11. W.I. Gillespie, "The Effect of Public Expenditures on the Distribution of Income: An Empirical Investigation" in *Essays in Fiscal Federalism* (R. Musgrave, ed.), Washington, D.C.: The Brookings Institution, 1971.

12. David A. Dodge, "Impact of Tax, Retransfer, and Expenditure Policies of Government on the Distribution of Personal Income in Canada," *Review of Income and Wealth* 21 (March 1975); and R.A. Musgrave, K.E. Case, H.B. Leonard, "The Distribution of Fiscal Burdens and Benefits," *Public Finance Quarterly* 2, no. 3 (July 1974).

13. U.S. Congress, House of Representatives, Intergovernmental Relations Subcommittee on Government Operations, *Federal Revenue and Expenditure Estimates for States and Regions, Fiscal Years 1965-67*, 90th Congress, Second Session. Washington, D.C.: U.S. Government Printing Office, October 1968.

14. Selma, Mushkin, "Distribution of Federal Taxes among the States," *National Tax Journal*, 9, no. 2, (June 1956); and "Distribution of Federal Expenditures among the States," *The Review of Economics and Statistics* 39, (November 1957).

15. *Allocating the Federal Tax Burden by State*, Research aid no. 3 (Revised), New York: Tax Foundation, Inc., 1964; and *Federal Tax Burdens in States and Metropolitan Areas*, Research aid no. 5, New York: Tax Foundation, Inc., April 1974.

16. Mushkin, "Distribution of Federal Expenditures," p. 436.

17. Ibid., p. 436.

18. Ibid., p. 438.

19. T.A. Stockfisch, "On the Obsolescence of Incidence," *Public Finance/Finances Publiques*, XIV (1959):148.

20. George F. Break, "The Incidence and Economic Effects of Taxation," in A.S. Blinder, R.M. Solow et al. *The Economics of Public Finance*, Washington, D.C.: The Brookings Institution, 1974, p. 124.

21. Stockfisch, "On the Obsolescence of Incidence," pp. 125-132.

22. R.A. Musgrave, *The Theory of Public Finance*, New York: McGraw-Hill, 1959, pp. 205-208.

23. Dodge, "Impact of Tax, Retransfer, and Expenditure Policies," p. 7.

24. The term is due to R. Musgrave and P. Musgrave, *Public Finance in Theory and Practice*, (2nd ed.) New York: McGraw-Hill, 1976, p. 388.

2

Federal Revenues: Personal Income, Corporate Income, Estate and Gift, and Payroll Taxes

Conceptual Incidence Theory

The Personal Income and Payroll Taxes

For the individual income tax there has always been wide consensus about its incidence in empirical estimation: the burden of the tax is borne by the individual on whom it is initially imposed. This is not to say that the reasoning behind this conclusion has been identical among all previous investigations. Some studies, like the routinely published reports of the Tax Foundation, have indicated that the incidence of the personal income tax is a more or less resolved issue, and that any exceptions will presumably be quantitatively unimportant. But other studies have recognized the possibility of shifting and have accepted this hypothesis on the basis of empirical evidence. Therefore, wherever there has been no discussion or supportive evidence, the generally accepted "nonshifting" hypothesis has been based on certain implicit assumptions regarding the factor supplies on one hand, and the effect of secondary changes on the other.

More specifically, if the personal income tax is assumed to rest with the individuals of the statutory liability, it is tacitly assumed that total factor supplies, labor and capital, are fixed. Furthermore, under a broad definition of incidence, there are three potential effects of progressive income taxes that, in principle, should be accounted for: (1) effect upon the demand for products, (2) effect upon savings, and (3) effect upon labor force participation.

Since the income tax raises more revenue from higher income classes, conceivably there could be a larger reduction in the demand for commodities consumed by wealthy households. To the extent, however, that the tax reduces only savings, the aggregate demand for consumption goods will be unaffected, although the resulting rise in the interest rate could increase the relative prices of capital-intensive commodities.

A progressive income tax involves a stronger substitution effect than an income effect, and labor force participation or work effort is adversely affected. However, even this conclusion no longer holds when all individuals are considered together. The final result will depend on the relative magnitudes of average and marginal rates, which are a function of the level of income.[1] It therefore becomes impossible to determine *a priori* the change in the total supply of work effort for the economy: it may increase, decrease, or remain unchanged. Any variation in the work effort will subsequently change the pretax

15

rates of returns for factors, as well as the relative product prices, which may give rise to further changes in the income position of households.

It is thus obvious that although some empirical evidence may be obtained regarding the first-order effects,[a] there is no way of allowing for the subsequent distribution changes in a meaningful manner—which precisely militates against the use of a broad definition of incidence, as explained in chapter 1.

Because of these limitations, the individual income tax has always been assumed to rest with the initial payee.[b] However, a closer look at the matter suggests that, even under the more narrow definition of incidence selected for this study (which implies a direct monetary transaction; see chapter 1, p. 11), the eventuality of shifting cannot be ruled out on *a priori* grounds. Within this framework the analysis may be developed according to three types of markets: (1) Perfect Competition, (2) Monopolistic Competition, and (3) Institutional Markets. This distinction is not always clear, and many elements are not necessarily mutually exclusive; it should therefore be understood to reflect only relative emphasis.

Perfect Competition. This case, which usually serves as the classical textbook example, has been extensively analyzed. As a result, it is not discussed in detail here. For the sake of theoretical completeness, however, note that (as is well known) a tax on income originating in a perfectly competitive market may stay put or be shifted forward, depending on the relative slopes of supply and demand schedules.

Monopolistic Competition. Of all the market types included in the general term "imperfect competition," only Monopolistic Competition appears suitable for discussion under the individual income tax. It is generally believed that, at least for the United States, it would be safer to postulate that firms operating in oligopolistic or monopolistic markets are incorporated businesses and consequently that their income would be subject to the corporate tax. Under this heading, therefore, one may classify the income of firms bearing the legal forms of proprietorships or partnerships, as well as the income from professional services, such as those of attorneys or doctors. The theoretical outcome of the shifting process is again uncertain. Consider figure 2-1.

---

[a]There is little empirical evidence that work effort is affected by the income tax, except in the case of young people and some women. See Marvin Kosters, "Effects of an Income Tax on Labor Supply," in A. Harberger and M. Baily (eds.), *The Taxation of Income from Capital*, Washington, D.C.: The Brookings Institution, 1969. There is also weak evidence that interest rates affect consumer saving. Colin Wright estimates the relevant elasticity in the range of 0.18 to 0.27. See his "Saving and the Rate of Interest," ibid.

[b]It is useful to point out at this juncture that under a *broad* definition of incidence the concept of tax shifting has been frequently confused with the notion of tax avoidance. However, there is a fundamental difference between these two ideas: the latter simply reflects a unilateral course of action, whereas the former necessarily implies a direct interaction between at least two parties.

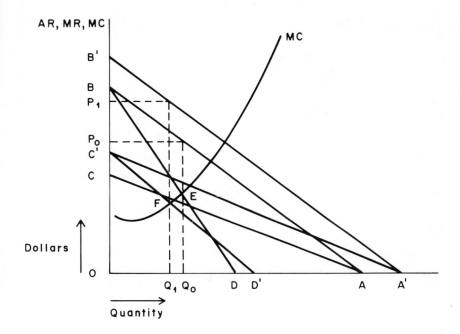

Note: The analysis describes the behavior of a producer of either a good or a service. To facilitate the diagrammatic exposition, the average cost and effective demand curves have been omitted.

Figure 2-1. Incidence of Personal Income Tax under Monopolistic Competition

The original equilibrium position is point E, where the MC curve intersects the marginal revenue curve BD corresponding to the original demand curve BA. The original price-quantity combination, therefore, is depicted by $0P_0$ and $0Q_0$, respectively.

The imposition of, or an increase in, the income tax will lower the slope of the demand schedule; the new (after-tax) curve may be thus represented by AC. The adjustment process continues, however, as individual firms contract output and some may cease operation. As output for the industry is reduced, the demand for the individual firm rises, for example, to $B'A'$. As a result, its new *net* (after-tax) schedule shifts to $C'A'$. The new equilibrium position is point F, where the MC curve intersects the new marginal revenue curve $C'D'$. Therefore, the new price is $0P_1$, and the new quantity $0Q_1$.

As can be clearly seen from figure 2-1, the increase in price is indeterminate: it may exceed or fall short of the tax, and as firms differ in their cost schedules, the change in the price may vary widely among individual producers.

Institutionalized Markets. This section is designed to cover the many hetero-geneous ramifications of the modern economy, whose unifying features are either collective bargaining or administered pricing, or both.[2]

In the case of collective bargaining, the income tax may well become part of the overall wage settlement. This assumes that, prior to tax, unions have asked for less than they are able to obtain. At any rate, such a response is not impossible, particularly in countries (for example, Sweden) where, under a highly centralized collective bargaining process, wage rates are set as part of a general incomes policy.

At the other end of the income scale, the compensation of executives is determined in a highly administered market. The compensation pattern depends on custom and general status considerations rather than on the precisely measured marginal productivity of the executives' services. In such a market, tax changes may well be reflected in changes in compensation designed to maintain desired patterns of after-tax remuneration.

Similar considerations arise with respect to capital income, where, inciden-tally, the assumption of a fixed supply of capital is a more serious theoretical limitation than that of labor. On a theoretical plane, therefore, the shifting of the individual income tax appears as a very real possibility. What comes to the salvation of empirical studies is some evidence that (one hopes) suggests that all these theoretical possibilities do not materialize in practice. For example, in the case of collective bargaining, unions have been observed to worry more about cost-of-living clauses than about tax-induced changes in take-home pay. Further-more, a study of executives' compensation has indicated that over a long period of time there has been no direct association between changes in salaries and changes in the tax rates of the corresponding brackets.[3] Finally, the extent of shifting, even in cases where it has been quantitatively appraised, is likely to be selective rather than general.

Hence, the overall conclusion remains that the burden of the individual income tax rests with those who bear the statutory liability. Nevertheless, one should not forget that this conclusion is due to a considerable degree to empirical limitations. Should quantitative results become available in the future, the traditional incidence assumption of the personal income tax may very well be revised.

The incidence of the payroll tax presents many similarities to that of the personal income tax. But it also poses some complications due to the statutory split of the contribution between employer and employee.

Under a system of competitive markets, a perfectly general payroll tax is borne entirely by the wage earner. Furthermore, most public finance experts accept the theorem that the economic effects of the tax are the same whether it is imposed on the employer or employee side of the labor market.[4]

Present federal payroll taxes, however, far from being related to competitive markets, are also not generally applicable and exclude nonmarket activities such as household work and leisure-time activities. From a practical point of view, the payroll tax may be considered to be "general," since coverage exceeds 90 percent of the U.S. labor force. (The notable exceptions are railroad and government employees, who have their own retirement plans.) But there remains the problem of market imperfections. At this point, the distinction between employers' and employees' contributions becomes important.

As far as the employees' contribution goes, the analysis is analogous to that presented earlier with respect to the personal income tax. In real terms, the question can be reduced to the relative strength of trade unions in their bargaining positions. In view, however, of the nearly universal nature of the tax, the employee half of the tax cannot be avoided: since there is practically no tax-free sector, the only escape would be to work less; but this is unlikely to be a major factor, because the supply of work effort has been found to be insensitive to income taxation.[5] This would be *a fortiori* the case for the payroll tax, which has much lower rates.

As far as the employers' contribution is concerned, there is much less agreement in the literature, because that portion of the tax is harder to analyze. Given the friction and institutional imperfections of markets, it has always been tacitly accepted by economists and laymen alike that the employer contribution is not likely to be absorbed by firms in reduced profits, but rather that it will be shifted in one way or another. Accordingly, attention has concentrated on the controversial issue regarding the direction of the shifting—backward or forward?

The question, to be sure, is more of academic than of practical significance, because the burden distribution is much the same whether we assume the tax to be borne by wage earners or by consumers.[6] Yet the eventuality of *forward* shifting is only a recent phenomenon. The earlier views were uniform in their acceptance of backward shifting as the only possibility. Indeed, some economists have expressed a virtually axiomatic belief that the employer portion of the payroll tax is borne by labor.

John Brittain reports an interesting case. In a letter to him welcoming preliminary statistical confirmation of this view, Milton Friedman remarked: "Indeed, I may say that if your statistical analysis had shown any other result, I would be inclined to regard that as a criticism of your statistical analysis, not as evidence against this particular proposition."[7]

Such one-sided opinions are no longer easy to discover. Many economists have expressed skepticism regarding the traditional conclusion that labor bears the entire tax burden. Why exactly this change occurred remains a mystery. By this we mean (at least to our knowledge) there has been no explicit theoretical proposition establishing that, once the desire for shifting on the part of the employer is taken for granted, forward shifting to consumers is a more reasonable proposition than backward shifting to labor. Perhaps the reason for the increasing willingness to accept the former view is the more or less intuitive presumption that, owing to the institutional rigidity of the labor market, it is easier for firms to shift their part of the tax by raising prices than by lowering money wages. There can be little doubt that the final answer must again be sought in empirical analysis.

In this respect, Brittain's monograph on the payroll tax is the established authoritative source of empirical findings. Using cross-section data for sixty-four countries and time-series data for the United States, he concluded that the employer portion of the tax is fully shifted to workers and that, therefore, the whole burden is borne by labor. In spite of certain debatable aspects of his investigation,[8] Brittain's careful econometric analysis offers substantial empirical evidence in favor of the backward-shifting hypothesis. From a theoretical point of view, he advances the proposition that the essence of his conclusion would not be altered if labor supply were elastic, provided that labor regarded both "contributions" as part of its supply price—that is, if labor thought of both taxes as part of earnings, just as they are definitely part of the employer's costs. Regardless of Brittain's findings, if payroll taxes are considered to be part of the employer's costs, labor is the most likely factor to bear the burden of the tax after the adjustment process has run its course. Undoubtedly, producers will tend to shift this levy, and may attempt to pass it on to consumers. But social security taxes are imposed on a nearly catholic basis; therefore, higher prices would simply reduce real incomes and cause a general reduction in effective demand. As a result, producers would be compelled to cut back on their demands for factors of production, the major impact being on labor.

The foregoing analysis, both theoretical and empirical, establishes that the most reasonable conclusion about the incidence of the payroll tax is that its full burden is borne by workers.

The Corporate Income Tax

What can you say about a levy whose history is marked by stubborn controversies? That it is important. And interesting. And still disputable. And that its name is "the corporate income tax."

This tax is surrounded by many intricate difficulties regarding its final "place of rest"—that is, its economic incidence. The principal, though by no means the only, controversy has centered around the hypothesis that the final burden is borne by some set of "capitalists" versus the alternative hypothesis that it is shifted, to a varying degree, forward to consumers. There can be little doubt that the corporate income tax has attracted a lot of attention not so much because of its economic significance,[c] but rather due to its important political

---

[c]Actually, in the year 1972 the corporate income tax as a source of revenue ranked fourth, next to the individual income tax, payroll tax, and the property tax. In terms of coverage, it accounted for only 52 percent of total capital income.

connotations, especially in a capitalistic economy such as that of the United States. The problem is that after so many years of research the issue remains controversial. For a clear understanding of the problem, one must distinguish between theoretical considerations and empirical evidence.

Theoretical Considerations. In the traditional view, a profit-maximizing firm, whether under competitive or monopolistic conditions, cannot shift the tax in the short run, because it has no incentive to change its optimum price-quantity combination. The general argument is that a tax on profits does not change the position of the marginal revenue and cost schedules; hence, it does not change the position of optimum price and output. Thus the tax cannot be shifted and lies solely on the stockholders.

A criticism of the traditional theory, at least in the case of a monopolist, may be centered around the definition of the concept of "profits," on which the corporate income tax is imposed. Profits, in a wide sense, are the sum of two components: "normal profits," which are part of the normal supply price; and "pure profits," which are over and above the normal profits. The implication of this distinction is that normal profits are incorporated in the marginal cost schedule of a firm; therefore, if the corporate tax does not allow for such profits, it is construed as a tax on costs. As a result, that portion of the tax which bears upon normal profits will be shifted. This is shown in figure 2-2 by a shifting of the original marginal cost curve upward to the new position indicated by MC'; hence, output is reduced from $0Q_0$ to $0Q_1$, and price rises from $0P_0$ to $0P_1$.

More important, however, than these qualifications of the traditional theory are a number of basic criticisms made of the assumptions underlying the whole marginalistic price theory. The criticisms may be grouped according to the alternative theories of the firm from which they arise.

Sales Maximization. The sales-maximization hypothesis has been advanced by W. Baumol[9] as an alternative to the traditional profit-maximization assumption. Since the corporate income tax does not change total sales as a function of price, simple sales maximization would again lead to the conclusion that the profits tax does not affect the optimum price-quantity combination.

But the firm is not likely to maximize sales while disregarding profits altogether. Most probably, its goal is to maximize sales subject to a minimum profit constraint. Defining the latter as net profits, we then have a behavior pattern that leads to shifting. Consider figure 2-3.

A sales-maximizing firm without constraint will be operating at the point where $MR = 0$, thus producing output $0Q_s$ at a price of $0P_s$. Still if the required profit is given by an area smaller than P_sABC, the sales-maximizing output $0Q_s$ will provide plenty of profit. If, however, the required minimum profit is larger—for example, given by area $P_cA'B'C'$—then the firm will reduce its output to $0Q_c$ and raise its price to $0P_c$.

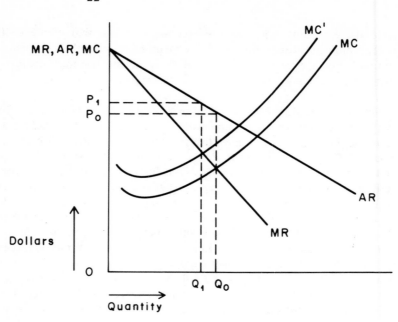

Figure 2-2. Incidence of Corporate Income Tax under Monopoly

Suppose that the firm requires minimum profit implied by output $0Q_c$ and price $0P_c$. If a profits tax of 50 percent is imposed, the firm will seek to double its profit in gross terms to net out the same amount as before. This is achieved by lowering its output $0Q_c$ and raising its price $0P_c$ (not shown in figure 2-3). The profit-maximizing output $0Q_p$ will always be smaller than the constrained output of a sales-maximizing firm, since at the point of profit maximization, marginal revenue is positive and the firm has an incentive to lower its price and increase its physical output. Obviously, if the required before-tax profit is greater than that implied by $0Q_p$, there is no output that will satisfy the constraint. In general, the application of corporate income tax to this model leads to partial shifting to the buyers of the products in the form of higher prices.

Markup Pricing. According to this approach, businesspeople set prices by calculating their average cost of production and then applying a markup representing their desired profit (including the return on invested capital). The markup thus becomes a percentage of the average cost of production. This situation is illustrated in figure 2-4.

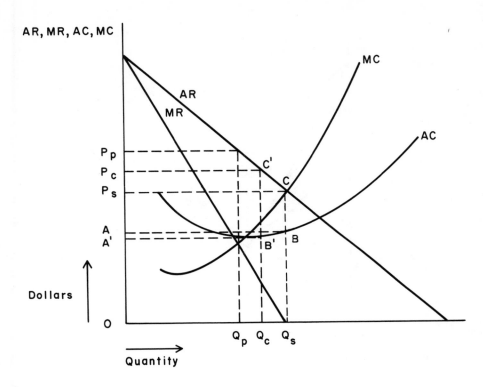

Figure 2-3. Incidence of Corporate Income Tax under Sales Maximization

The profit maximizing output and price are, respectively, $0Q_p$ and $0P_p$ and are not affected by the imposition of a corporate tax. If the producer is a markup price setter, however, he applies a percentage markup to his AC curve, leading to AC' as his basis for the quantity decision. Then he will choose to produce $0Q_b$ and sell it at $0P_b$.

Now, suppose that a corporate income tax is imposed on the markup pricer. If the producer treats his tax liability as another fixed cost of production, he may add it to his other fixed and variable costs of production, and thus derive a new average-cost curve such as AC''. This will lead to a lower output $0Q_a$, and a higher price $0P_a$, which implies a partial shifting to consumers in the producer's attempt to incorporate his tax liability into the markup formula.

Other Pricing Rules. Analogous reasoning may be developed for many other market imperfections or, more generally, for the entire category of pricing behavior known as "administered pricing." The basic idea is that, in one way or another, the corporate income tax is likely to be shifted, even if the observer is

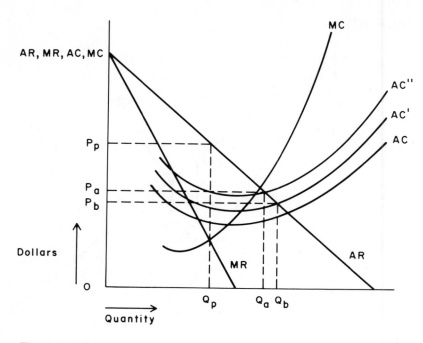

Figure 2-4. Incidence of Corporate Income Tax under Markup Pricing

uncertain about the price type of market in which the firm operates. In the words of one businessman: "Corporate taxes are simply costs, and the method of their assessment does not change this fact. Costs must be paid by the public in prices, and corporate taxes are thus in effect concealed sales taxes."[10]

As the foregoing presentation clearly demonstrates, one can draw whatever conclusion one likes from theoretical debates. Hence, unless an argument can be based on empirical facts, any *a priori* conclusion on the incidence of the corporate income tax is bound to fail.

Empirical Evidence. Several models are the principal means of gathering empirical evidence.

Short-Run Models. The best known model was developed by Krzyzaniak and Musgrave (K-M for short).[11] They focused on the rate of return earned on capital, and they argued that to the extent that the tax is shifted, before-tax profit rates will rise as firms fully or partly restore their after-tax profit rates to their former levels. Shifting is measured by the regression coefficients between the rates of return and of the tax. Using data from the manufacturing sector, K-M concluded that the corporate income tax was shifted more than 100 percent and, in one case, up to 134 percent. Despite the authors' disclaimers that their measure was not only one of tax incidence, but was contaminated by influences of budget incidence, K-M's results were received very critically by the profession. The basic objection has been that the tax variable also captures the effects of cyclical and wartime phenomena on profit rates.

In an attempt to avoid the inconsistencies of the K-M study, R.J. Gordon employed a different specification and a different method of estimation and concluded that the parameter of tax shifting is not significantly different from zero.[12] Gordon's results were based on the hypothesis that firms practice markup pricing; his model included productivity as an input and thus obtained consistent tax shifting coefficients relative to both the rate of return and the income share. Gordon's critique has been refuted by K-M. They state that he fails to integrate satisfactorily the tax variable into a structural system as part of the price equation.

In yet another attempt to determine the degree of shifting, Challis Hall used a production function approach along traditional lines.[13] He based his model on marginal productivity theory and, in contrast to the K-M method and the Gordon approach, he included variables to account for the effects of changes in the capital-labor ratio and of the technical change on the return to capital. He concluded that the no-shift hypothesis yields an equation with the highest coefficient of determination (R^2). R. Musgrave, however, has questioned the validity of making inferences about shifting on the basis of small variations in R^2.

Long-Run Models.[d] In 1962 A. Harberger published his now classic analysis on the incidence of the corporate income tax.[14] Harberger uses an elegant methodology to study the long-run incidence of the corporate tax. His paper, although organizationally exemplary, can provide a basis for empirical analysis only on acceptance of the following crucial assumptions: (1) perfect competition in all industries, (2) perfect mobility of factors between sectors, (3) demand elasticities equal to one, and (4) inelastic supply of savings. Harberger's model is a good starting point, but his critics have attacked the assumptions of perfect mobility and perfect competition. At any rate, Harberger's basic conclusion is that the burden of this tax is borne by all capitalists as a group.

In this sense, the analysis by J.G. Cragg, A.C. Harberger, and Peter Mieszkowski (C-H-M for short) is more readily acceptable.[15] Their object is to estimate the long-run incidence of the corporate tax within the Krzyzaniak-

---

[d]Strictly speaking, these works are not directly relevant for our purpose, since we have adopted a "short-run" definition of incidence. They are included here, however, for reasons of theoretical completeness in this important area.

Musgrave framework, while simultaneously criticizing the latters' specification. Adding the unemployment rate and a dummy variable to the K-M model to capture the influence of cyclical and wartime phenomena, C-H-M conclude that total capital, incorporated and unincorporated, bore the full burden of the tax.

Finally, an algorithmic approach to the problem has been advanced by Shoven and Whalley, based on a procedure developed by H. Scarf for calculating general equilibrium prices in a competitive setting.[16] Using the same data as Harberger, but relaxing the linearity assumptions as well as that of constant factor supplies, Shoven and Whalley conclude that, in most cases, capital bears the full burden of the corporate tax. Their results corroborate Harberger's findings by demonstrating that his conclusions are correct, even after certain basic assumptions have been relaxed. Unfortunately, the assumption of perfect competition was not tested by Shoven and Whalley, and in this respect nothing can be said one way or another.

The studies mentioned in the foregoing discussion may be reasonably regarded as the major ones in the history of econometric research on the incidence of the corporate income tax, but there exist many other investigations as well, all of which lead to the conclusion that the overall picture is far from clear. For example, a 1970 study by Joan Turek, elaborating on the production function approach adopted by Challis Hall, concludes that there is practically no shifting, whereas a 1972 investigation by Richard Dusansky, based on the rate of return approach, shows 100 percent forward shifting.[17]

What, then, can you say about a levy whose history is marked by stubborn controversies? Essentially that "politicians may be able to sell a corporate tax increase simultaneously to workers and consumers who think it would mainly burden capitalists and to capitalists and businessmen who think it would mainly burden consumers."[18]

This is, of course, a very eloquent way of summarizing the problem, and one that suggests no other empirical solution but the use of the most important alternative hypotheses in the estimation of the corporate tax burden. Therefore, the following four alternative incidence assumptions are employed in this study: (1) incidence on consumers of corporate products, (2) incidence on corporate capital (no shifting), (3) incidence on capital at large, and (4) incidence on labor in the corporate sector.

Estate and Gift Taxes

There is little controversy over the incidence of estate and gift taxes. Since they cannot be shifted, it may be assumed that the burden of these taxes is borne by decedents and donors.

Ideal Measures and Estimation of Burden Distribution by State

The Personal Income and Payroll Taxes

In accordance with the incidence assumptions adopted earlier, the ideal measures of distribution of the personal and the payroll tax are the respective tax liabilities of residents. In the case of these taxes, therefore, the estimated distribution by state coincides with the ideal measurement. Data were obtained from direct sources (see end of table 2-1) with some minor modifications.

The Corporate Income Tax

In conformity with the four incidence assumptions adopted for the corporate income tax, the ideal measures of distribution would be as follows:

1. If the tax is shifted forward to consumers, the ideal basis would be the geographical distribution of consumption of corporate products.
2. If only corporate capital bears the burden of the tax, however, then the ideal series would be the distribution of capital income originating in the corporate sector by state.
3. If capital at large bears the full burden of the tax, the ideal basis would be the distribution of capital income by state.
4. Finally, if the tax is shifted backward to labor, the burden would have to be allocated according to labor income originating in the corporate sector by
   . state.

The available data on dividend income, interest income, and unincorporated business income provide an adequate statistical basis for a sound estimation of the corporate income tax under the first two assumptions.[e] The third incidence assumption poses certain serious complications. First, estimates of actual consumption are nonexistent, save for an extremely small number of commodities (for example, tobacco products and alcoholic beverages). Therefore,

---

[e]An alternative distributive series could be the geographical dispersion of wealth. This has the theoretical attraction of capturing capital gains, but its applicability in practice is not advisable on account of two limitations: First, wealth estimates would have been obtained by using estate tax returns and, strictly speaking, these would have been valid only for households with gross assets of $60,000 or more. Second, and more important for our purposes, the estimates of tax burden based on the incidence assumptions that require wealth figures would not have been comparable with the rest, as the former would have used a "stock" variable (wealth), whereas the latter a "flow" variable (consumption or labor income).

use of retail sales as a proxy of consumption expenditures is inevitable. Second, no data are available that distinguish sales of corporate products from the pattern of general sales. If we assume that the pattern of retail trade reflects the sales of corporate products, then data on retail trade by state provide the necessary information for the regional allocation of the corporate income tax. Without making this rather strong assumption, there appears to be no other method of allocating the revenues from this tax in accordance with the third assumption.

The empirical estimation of the final incidence assumption constitutes one of the most difficult problems encountered in the present study. Regionally disaggregated data, either direct or indirect, are not available. By "direct" we mean data on corporate payrolls by region; by "indirect" we mean a combination of several proxy variables that, upon a suitable transformation, could generate corporate payrolls. (Remember that a single, uniformly applied, transformation is inadequate, because it is bound to disappear as soon as normalization of the data occurs.)

Since estimates of the split between corporate and noncorporate payrolls are unavailable, the empirical allocation is based on two alternative methods: distribution by total payroll, and distribution by manufacturing payroll. The latter series may be thought of as a *prima facie* proxy for corporate payrolls, whereas the former can be rationalized by assuming that there is no systematic bias in corporate payrolls as a percentage of total payrolls across geographical regions. (This assumption, of course, does not preclude differentiation in corporate payrolls *by industry* across the states.)

Estate and Gift Taxes

As mentioned earlier, the burden of these taxes is assumed to stay put. For the case of estate taxes, one might argue that the burden falls equally on inheritors. Unfortunately, no data are available indicating the geographical distribution of this group. Since estate and gift taxes together amount to less than 3 percent of federal revenues, the results would be little affected by this alternative incidence assumption.

Table 2-1 presents estimates of the distribution of the tax burden by state in 1972 for the personal income, the payroll, and estate and gift taxes. Similarly, table 2-2 provides alternative estimates of the distribution of the tax burden by state for the corporate income tax under the five different methods.

Table 2-1
State Allocation of Tax Burden for Personal Income, Payroll, and Estate and Gift Taxes, 1972
(in millions of dollars)

	Personal Income Tax	Payroll Tax	Estate and Gift Tax
Alabama	$1,031.61	$843.13	$35.41
Alaska	174.04	162.03	1.18
Arizona	833.66	562.09	38.86
Arkansas	512.72	437.07	17.49
California	9,606.22	6,190.99	731.17
Colorado	1,088.64	668.11	53.96
Connecticut	1,949.48	1,118.18	155.32
Delaware	325.42	219.04	16.31
District of Columbia	404.11	437.07	14.02
Florida	3,585.26	2,005.32	356.43
Georgia	1,782.90	1,381.22	96.50
Hawaii	416.40	281.04	14.67
Idaho	221.03	194.03	16.66
Illinois	6,318.92	3,704.59	379.37
Indiana	2,365.39	1,674.27	89.78
Iowa	1,093.85	793.13	72.98
Kansas	899.50	518.08	54.25
Kentucky	1,098.58	762.12	53.46
Louisiana	1,162.68	812.13	55.60
Maine	300.12	237.04	24.07
Maryland	2,297.59	1,143.18	109.20
Massachusetts	2,872.01	1,668.27	190.93
Michigan	4,614.76	2,986.48	160.04
Minnesota	1,504.03	1,143.18	73.58
Mississippi	532.37	481.08	22.19
Missouri	2,014.56	1,406.23	130.37
Montana	227.12	175.03	18.79
Nebraska	596.23	431.07	44.53
Nevada	303.35	175.03	30.22
New Hampshire	345.26	231.04	18.56
New Jersey	4,381.74	2,467.39	227.13
New Mexico	319.99	237.04	18.39
New York	9,674.29	6,754.08	641.01
North Carolina	1,819.14	1,624.26	81.63
North Dakota	165.30	137.02	8.38
Ohio	5,005.61	3,217.52	255.85
Oklahoma	907.66	637.10	42.51

Table 2-1 (cont.)

	Personal Income Tax	Payroll Tax	Estate and Gift Tax
Oregon	948.25	681.11	48.54
Pennsylvania	5,322.93	3,810.61	273.54
Rhode Island	403.95	300.05	22.69
South Carolina	829.02	750.12	29.03
South Dakota	161.68	150.02	9.64
Tennessee	1,419.96	1,174.19	89.57
Texas	4,712.01	3,111.50	293.63
Utah	355.32	300.05	9.29
Vermont	163.85	131.02	9.52
Virginia	2,210.30	1,256.20	94.84
Washington	1,520.27	993.16	66.59
West Virginia	603.73	431.07	29.99
Wisconsin	1,819.11	1,362.22	100.49
Wyoming	131.87	100.02	7.82
All States	$93,353.77	$62,467.00	$5,436.00

Sources: Table compiled by the author. Original data from *Individual Income Tax Returns* (U.S. Department of the Treasury, Internal Revenue Service, various years); *Social Security Bulletin, Annual Statistical Supplement* (U.S. Department of Health, Education, and Welfare, Social Security Administration, 1972); *Fiduciary, Gift, and Estate Tax Returns* (U.S. Department of the Treasury, Internal Revenue Service, various years); *Defense Personnel and Total Population in the United States by State* (U.S. Department of Defense, Office of Assistant Secretary, 1974, unpublished); *Survey of Current Business* (U.S. Department of Commerce, Office of Business Economics, various issues); and *Annual Report of the Commissioner of the Internal Revenue Service* (U.S. Department of the Treasury, Internal Revenue Service 1972 and 1973).

Note: Details may not add to totals due to rounding.

Table 2-2
State Allocation of Tax Burden for the Corporate Income Tax, 1972
(in millions of dollars)

	Allocation by:				
	Total Retail Trade[a]	Dividend Income[b]	Total Capital Income[c]	Manufacturing Payroll[d]	Total Payroll[d]
Alabama	$461.13	$219.59	$290.25	$437.56	$381.45
Alaska	54.04	10.87	28.49	11.44	38.21
Arizona	333.61	279.45	224.62	166.27	267.05
Arkansas	274.02	183.85	286.99	208.54	186.85
California	3,424.61	3,541.45	2,824.82	2,850.87	3,363.93
Colorado	411.08	291.56	433.57	230.67	338.00
Connecticut	505.52	908.47	530.20	716.11	591.18

Table 2-2 (cont.)

	Total Retail Trade[a]	Dividend Income[b]	Total Capital Income[c]	Manufacturing Payroll[d]	Total Payroll[d]
			Allocation by:		
Delaware	103.69	209.66	96.64	147.13	112.54
District of Columbia	125.87	180.37	101.31	42.98	192.81
Florida	1,380.34	2,110.70	1,156.07	490.95	962.61
Georgia	729.27	460.89	454.14	621.62	651.49
Hawaii	130.63	131.77	102.79	36.70	114.27
Idaho	116.28	46.07	172.73	63.17	74.94
Illinois	1,815.69	2,055.05	2,403.09	2,360.22	2,194.37
Indiana	803.22	539.45	801.49	1,258.89	876.47
Iowa	411.62	246.43	1,438.60	365.89	335.56
Kansas	333.80	259.81	828.79	211.23	242.58
Kentucky	431.53	293.74	425.98	389.49	362.05
Louisiana	505.27	318.41	370.23	284.44	422.50
Maine	156.42	195.12	123.41	128.82	114.65
Maryland	664.00	645.03	478.90	445.03	543.13
Massachusetts	931.46	1,152.58	728.20	1,047.60	1,054.97
Michigan	1,444.98	1,371.28	1,064.72	2,375.15	1,668.27
Minnesota	585.02	426.06	816.52	530.49	568.29
Mississippi	277.47	142.93	210.48	226.71	196.79
Missouri	719.48	708.79	896.38	729.84	749.79
Montana	113.04	61.20	185.99	35.87	63.51
Nebraska	223.75	153.12	867.94	125.73	172.46
Nevada	110.15	78.35	39.95	15.01	94.67
New Hampshire	142.78	143.35	100.21	120.67	104.82
New Jersey	1,178.90	1,599.00	1,135.61	1,476.20	1,299.23
New Mexico	161.12	109.46	83.80	31.07	100.46
New York	2,743.77	4,365.09	2,882.15	3,110.06	3,739.94
North Carolina	745.98	577.56	697.07	900.05	720.26
North Dakota	89.30	36.01	384.49	12.81	47.23
Ohio	1,603.22	1,502.06	1,363.80	2,510.29	1,884.96
Oklahoma	387.12	220.18	385.53	206.11	291.46
Oregon	363.56	245.75	348.80	291.79	303.41
Pennsylvania	1,763.79	2,109.18	1,598.96	2,379.34	1,998.21
Rhode Island	141.36	197.11	107.41	164.34	144.32
South Carolina	362.40	191.99	238.87	427.44	316.18
South Dakota	92.15	33.23	232.38	23.83	48.64
Tennessee	592.98	348.02	386.09	632.48	544.99
Texas	1,809.39	1,333.46	1,613.58	1,182.25	1,546.06
Utah	167.00	96.60	92.10	82.76	124.81

Table 2-2 (cont.)

	Allocation by:				
	Total Retail Trade[a]	Dividend Income[b]	Total Capital Income[c]	Manufacturing Payroll[d]	Total Payroll[d]
Vermont	77.26	82.72	49.12	58.20	58.88
Virginia	702.52	639.37	474.33	516.39	572.02
Washington	524.96	376.17	638.92	407.36	455.14
West Virginia	231.60	189.73	160.17	207.53	227.45
Wisconsin	650.72	500.77	752.36	860.37	667.87
Wyoming	57.15	47.14	56.94	10.23	34.25
All States	$32,166.00	$32,166.00	$32,166.00	$32,166.00	$32,166.00

Sources: Table computed by the author. Original data from *Individual Income Tax Returns* (U.S. Department of the Treasury, Internal Revenue Service, various years); and *County Business Patterns* (U.S. Department of Commerce, Social and Economic Statistics Administration, Bureau of the Census, various years).

Note: Details may not add to totals due to rounding.

[a]Incidence on consumers. See text for details.

[b]Incidence on owners of corporate capital. See text for details.

[c]Incidence on owners of capital at large. See text for details.

[d]Incidence on workers. See text for explanation and details.

Notes

1. R. Musgrave, *Theory of Public Finance,* pp. 243-246.

2. This section draws on Musgrave and Musgrave, *Public Finance,* pp. 387-388.

3. See W.G. Lewellen, "An Intersectoral Analysis of Senior Executive Rewards," *Proceedings of the National Tax Association,* October, 1969.

4. The theorem is summarized in R. Musgrave, *Theory of Public Finance,* pp. 350-352.

5. See Kosters, "Effects of an Income Tax on Labor Supply."

6. This view is explicitly put forward by at least two incidence studies. See Musgrave and Musgrave, *Public Finance,* pp. 366-372, and Tax Foundation, *Federal Tax Burdens,* p. 17.

7. John A. Brittain, *The Payroll Tax for Social Security,* Studies of Government Finance. Washington, D.C.: The Brookings Institution, 1972, p. 22.

8. Some of these aspects are summarized in Break, "Economic Effects of Taxation," pp. 169-173. Further discussion may be found in M.S. Feldstein and J. Brittain, "The Incidence of the Social Security Tax: Comment and Reply," *American Economic Review* 62 (September 1972).

9. W. Baumol, *Economic Theory and Operations Analysis,* (4th ed.), Englewood Cliffs, N.J.: Prentice-Hall, 1976, p. 387.

10. E.M. Voorhees, U.S. Steel Corporation, reported in the *New York Times*, October 10, 1943.

11. M. Krzyzaniak, and R. Musgrave, *The Shifting of the Corporation Income Tax*, Baltimore: Johns Hopkins Press, 1963.

12. R.J. Gordon, "The Incidence of the Corporation Income Tax in U.S. Manufacturing," *American Economic Review* 57 (September 1967).

13. C.A. Hall, Jr., "Direct Shifting of the Corporation Income Tax in Manufacturing," *American Economic Review* 54 (May 1964).

14. A.C. Harberger, "The Incidence of the Corporation Income Tax," *Journal of Political Economy* 70 (June 1962).

15. J.C. Cragg, A.C. Harberger and P. Mieszkowski, "Empirical Evidence on the Incidence of the Corporation Income Tax," *Journal of Political Economy* 75 (December 1967).

16. J.B. Shoven and J. Whalley, "A General Equilibrium Calculation of the Effects of Differential Taxation of Income from Capital in the United States" *Journal of Public Economics* 1 (November 1972).

17. Joan Turek, "Short-Run Shifting of the Corporate Income Tax in Manufacturing, 1935-1965," *Yale Economic Essays* (Spring 1970); Richard Dusansky, "The Short-Run Shifting of the Corporation Income Tax in the United States," *Oxford Economic Papers* (November 1972).

18. Break, "Economic Effects of Taxation," p. 154.

3 Federal Revenues: Selective Sales Taxes and Customs Duties

Conceptual Incidence Theory

Selective sales taxes and customs duties constitute the general category of excise taxes or, simply, excises. Although the unqualified use of the term "excise" is usually understood to relate to a tax rather than to a duty, these two forms of taxation are conceptually equivalent, and in this section the expression "excise taxes" is meant to refer to both of them, unless an explicit distinction is made.

Excise taxation has always played a very important role in government finances, although not so great in the United States as in other countries. Customs duties, in particular, are one of the most ancient forms of taxation. During the Middle Ages and the mercantilistic era, they were as a rule the state's most important source of revenue. Today, under the influence of international movements for the establishment of customs unions and free-trade areas, their revenue has declined both in relative and in absolute terms. Some people believe that customs duties are nowadays an instrument of foreign policy and that their role as a tool of taxation has all but disappeared.[1] At any rate, customs duties and selective sales taxes together amounted to slightly less than 8 percent of general revenues for the year 1972.

The variety of excises levied by the federal government is indeed bewildering. They range from the chief categories of alcohol, tobacco, and gasoline to items such as firearms, wagers, narcotics, and matches. Such a diversification would immediately suggest that the burden of these taxes is likely to be shifted differentially. It therefore emerges as a pleasant surprise that there is wide consensus about the incidence of excise taxes. There is general agreement that excise taxes are shifted forward to consumers of the taxed commodities, and in what follows we analyze why this is not only a reasonable proposition but also the most likely outcome of the market mechanism.

From the historical point of view, the primary reason for the wide application of excises has been that these are normally easy to collect in practice. Subsequently, social considerations played a major part in shaping excise taxation. First, equity reasons created the desire to tax luxury goods. Second, the increasing understanding of the difference between social and private costs led to the introduction of the so-called *sumptuary* taxes on commodities that are considered socially or morally undesirable. Third, the same argument has been used in favor of *regulatory* excises for the improvement of the allocation of resources, although their practical importance is minimal, because the U.S. Congress has strongly resisted the passing of pertinent legislation. Finally, the benefit principle of taxation provided the conceptual basis for the establishment of *user charges,* which are taxes whose proceeds are used to pay for particular services provided by government to consumers.

All of the components of the preceding analysis point to the conclusion that the intention of the legislator is, for one reason or another, to affect final consumption via excise taxation. We may therefore divide excise taxes into two categories: (1) those whose statutory incidence rests directly with consumers, but which, for reasons of simplicity, are collected by the producer of the taxable good or service; and (2) those whose statutory incidence rests with the producer, but for which the intended and desired incidence is linked with consumers. Prime examples in the first category are Telephone and Teletype Services, Transportation of Persons by Air, and Use of International Air Travel Facilities.[2] The second category includes virtually all other excises, which reflect the bulk of federal revenues.

The main conceptual difficulty, of course, relates to the second group and, in particular, to the eventuality that, the legislator's intention notwithstanding, the forces of the market may be such as to impede full forward shifting. The question therefore arises, to what extent are excise taxes that are statutorily levied on producers shifted to consumers?

In theory, the answer depends on the magnitudes of the slopes of the demand and supply curves. Since the initial effect of an excise tax is either a vertical shift in the demand curve in the case of a unit tax, or a change in the slope of the curve in the case of an *ad valorem* tax, the burden of excise taxes in general is borne in part by the consumers and in part by the producers of the taxed commodity. This is shown diagrammatically in figure 3-1, under perfect competition and monopoly, for the more realistic case of an *ad valorem* tax.[a]

In both cases the imposition of the excise tax results in an increase of the original price and a decrease of the original output. Under perfect competition, the supply curve S intersects the before-tax demand schedule at point E_1 with corresponding price $0P_1$ and output $0Q_1$. Imposition of an *ad valorem* tax swivels the net average revenue (demand) schedule to D_2. The new intersection of supply and demand is point E_2, which corresponds to $Q_2 < Q_1$ and $P_2 > P_1$. In the case of monopoly, the tax changes the slope of both the average and marginal revenue schedules. The pretax price is $0P_1$ and output is $0Q_1$. After the tax is imposed, price rises to $0P_2$ and output falls to $0Q_2$.

As inspection of figure 3-1 shows, if demand is relatively inelastic, most of the incidence is borne by the consumer; if supply is relatively inelastic, the

---

[a]Most excises are levied on an *ad valorem* basis—that is, as a percentage of the value of output. Also, an excise tax may be viewed as either an addition to average cost or a reduction in average revenue. For the case of an *ad valorem* tax, it is more straightforward to describe the changes in terms of the demand curve. Finally, it is reminded that this analysis holds for both selective excise taxes and customs duties, and that by the term "producer" we also mean the "distributor" of a given product.

37

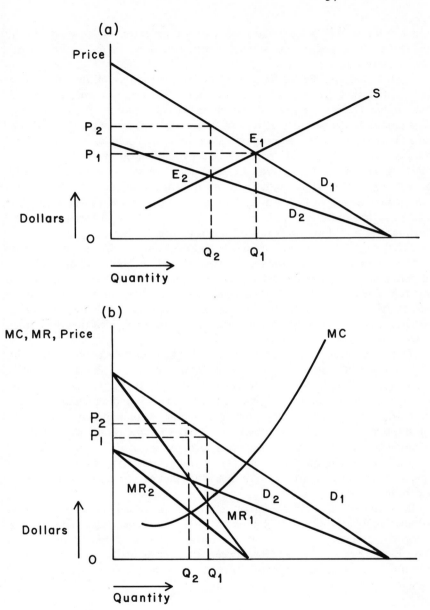

Figure 3-1. Incidence of *Ad Valorem* Tax
(a) Under Perfect Competition
(b) Under Monopoly

burden is borne mainly by the producer. Hence, empirical evidence on demand (and to a lesser degree, on supply) constitutes a *prima facie* case for the incidence of excise taxation.

Houthakker and Taylor have analyzed the demand conditions for several commodities that are subject to excise taxes. Their econometric evidence is based upon equations estimated for individual expenditure items using time series data from the period 1929-1963.[3] Their estimates of the price elasticity of demand are low and statistically insignificant for "alcoholic beverages," for "gasoline and oil," and for "new cars and net purchases of used cars," all of which amounted to 62 percent of total selective sales revenues for 1972. However, they report a statistically significant price elasticity (−.26) for "telephone, telegraph and wireless" services and, somewhat surprisingly, a substantial long-run price elasticity (−1.89) of demand for "tobacco products," which represented almost one-fifth of total revenues.

Interpreted literally, this evidence suggests that the incidence of excise taxation is borne by consumers in the case of alcohol, motor fuel, and automobiles. In contrast, the incidence of excises on tobacco products and communications may fall partly on consumers and partly on producers. In the absence of evidence on the supply elasticities, it is assumed that the supply elasticities for tobacco products and communications are so high that the burden of taxation is borne by consumers.

This assumption ought to be viewed in the light of the existing conformity of opinions that the objective of excise taxation is to place the burden of the tax on consumers. G.F. Break and J.A. Pechman have recently repeated their belief that excises fall on consumers "since they are usually levied on items consumed by a large proportion of the low and middle income population, whose consumption is not very sensitive to price."[4] Despite the econometric evidence presented by Houthakker and Taylor in favor of some moderate elasticity of demand for certain products, the overwhelming majority of public finance experts seems to adhere to the traditional tenet that excises are ultimately borne by consumers.

In summary, the present study assumes that selective sales taxes and customs duties are fully shifted forward to the consumers of taxed products. Owing to the involved methodology employed for the geographical distribution of excise taxes, we distinguish between the conceptually ideal method of allocation and the actual estimation procedure. These topics are treated in turn in the next two sections.

Ideal Measures of Distribution

As was briefly mentioned in the first chapter, the treatment of excise taxes has been the weakest aspect of all previous studies of fiscal incidence. The single most important oversight has been the failure to distinguish between commodities used almost exclusively in final consumption and those used also as intermediate goods. For, even under the assumption of full forward shifting, the burden of excises levied on intermediate goods will necessarily fall on a wider variety of consumers than those who consume the goods only in direct final consumption. Therefore, unless the estimation is based on such a distinction, the results are likely to be inadequate and perhaps misleading.

Such a separation is not strictly binary; in other words, some goods which may be classified as "intermediate" are also used in final consumption. But a considerable portion of their output is used as an input in other sectors, thus warranting a special methodological procedure. Therefore, the term "intermediate" goods should not be interpreted in a strictly literal sense.

Once the distinction between "final" and "intermediate" taxable or dutiable commodities has been made, then, in view of the incidence assumption adopted earlier, the former category may be allocated across regions on the basis of the respective consumption patterns. But for the latter group it is necessary to use information on the interindustry structure of the economy. This information, which is found in an Input-Output (I-O) table of the economy, may accordingly be utilized as follows.

First, a comparison between "personal consumption expenditures" and "total intermediate outputs" provides an objective criterion for classifying the goods as "final" or "intermediate." If the grouping has been made on some other basis, this comparison checks the previous classification.

Subsequently, the I-O table may be used to obtain the weights for prorating the tax revenues from "intermediate" goods.

Consider a taxable industry $w(1)$.

Then, for any given processing industry $w(j)$, $j = 1, \ldots, N$, the "total value" of $w(1)$ used directly or indirectly as input in $w(j)$ is equal to

the coefficient of total requirements of $w(1)$ per unit of final demand of $w(j)$	$\times$	personal consumption expenditures on $w(j)$

Notice that the use of the total requirements coefficient ensures that the full interdependence among industries is taken into account. Also notice that the use of personal consumption expenditures in the preceding product reflects the assumption that the tax incidence is borne by the household sector.

We thus obtain a row vector corresponding to $w(1)$ and representing its "total value" in each industry $w(j)$. The procedure may then be repeated for every other industry $w(i)$, $i = 2, \ldots, M$, until we have exhausted the number of taxable industries. Hence, we finally obtain a complete set of "total values" of each taxable industry $w(i)$ for every processing industry $w(j)$, which can subsequently be used as weights for the allocation of tax revenues. The weights must of course be coupled with the corresponding consumption patterns across geographical regions.

This is a very schematic representation of the ideal methodology for the regional allocation of excise taxes and, in particular, of those levied on "intermediate" commodities. But for this procedure to become operational, several modifications are needed in practice. First, the large number of selective excises and customs duties make it necessary to aggregate many commodities into broader groups of taxable goods. Second, even after this aggregation, the existing I-O tables of the U.S. economy are not sufficiently detailed for a direct focus on the desired commodities. It is therefore necessary to identify the I-O industries that correspond to the set of "intermediate" taxable or dutiable commodities, and to match them. If it turns out that one industry corresponds to more than one commodity, we are then required to make the assumption that the individual products identified with a certain industry follow the same pattern of distribution as the industry itself—that is, that the industry is an accurate "cross section" of its individual components. Finally, for the over-whelming majority of products there is no available information on actual consumption; as a result, the use of retail sales data as a proxy for consumption expenditures appears inevitable. Therefore, the final step is the matching of the weights—that is, of the processing industries that correspond to each taxable or dutiable industry—with retail sales outlets.

The details of this procedure, together with some technical restrictions that are unavoidable because of practical considerations, are presented in the next section.

Estimation of Burden Distribution by State

Selective Sales Taxes

In 1972 the major sources of sales and gross receipts revenues were as shown in table 3-1. That only four taxes contribute more than 10 percent each to total revenues suggests that even this classification, although substantially general compared to the actual number of excises, is too detailed for analytical purposes. Therefore, it was decided to use the following level of detail, which contributes to analytical clarity and lends itself to easier interpretation, as well.

		Percent of Total Revenues
1.	Alcoholic beverages	31
2.	Petroleum products	26
3.	Tobacco products	13

	Percent of *Total Revenues*
4. Communications	10
5. Truck and bus bodies	4
6. Tires and Tubes	4
7. Motor vehicles	3
8. Sugar	1
9. Use tax on highways	1
10. Other excise taxes	7

Of these categories alcoholic beverages and tobacco products are unquestionably "final" products, and the tax revenues are consequently allocated directly on the basis of final consumption. Here there is no need to use retail sales as a proxy, because direct estimates of consumption are available by state (see end of table 3-5 for the relevant sources).

Before proceeding to the analysis of excises levied on "intermediate" goods,

Table 3-1
Sources of Major Excise Tax Revenues, 1972

Type of Tax	*Percent of Total Excise Revenues*
Distilled spirits	22
Gasoline	22
Cigarettes	13
Telephone and teletype	10
Beer	7
Motor vehicles, chassis, bodies, parts, accessories	7
Tires, tubes, rubber	4
Transportation of persons by air	3
Diesel and special motor fuel	2
Wines, cordials	1
Use tax on highway motor vehicles	1
Sugar	<1
Lubricating oil	<1
Cigars	<1
Use of international air facilities	<1
Use tax on civil aircraft	<1
Noncommercial aviation gasoline	<1
Noncommercial aviation fuel other than gasoline	<1
All other taxes	2

Source: *Annual Report of the Commissioner of the Internal Revenue Service* (U.S. Department of the Treasury, Internal Revenue Service, 1972 and 1973).

it is important to emphasize that the research strategy for this group was based on the recurring tradeoffs between accumulating a massive but unmalleable body of data on the one hand, and interpreting a less exhaustive but more sharply focused investigation on the other. Because of the large number of detailed methodological steps employed at the various stages, a great part of the procedures, together with the relevant criteria and a brief analysis of the decision-making process, are explained in the appendixes A-B, which the interested reader should consult. In the text below, as a rule, only the final conclusions of the research strategy are presented.

For those levies imposed on "intermediate" goods the problem was managed by using the 1967 Input-Output (I-O) tables published by the U.S. Department of Commerce.[5] The tables are based on a 367-industry classification, and the first step was the identification of the industries that correspond to the individual taxed commodities. The correspondence shown in table 3-2 was arrived at.

The next step involves the utilization of the I-O table to obtain the "total values" that should be used as weights for the allocation of tax revenues. A computer program was developed to carry out the computation of "total values" as described in the previous section (p. 39). The program ranked the I-O industries according to the contribution to their respective "values" of a given taxed industry. Not surprisingly, many elements in each of the seven vectors turned out to be negligible. For all cases 80 percent of the total contribution was reflected in fewer than thirty industries. In two cases, namely "sugar" and

Table 3-2
Correspondence between Taxable Commodities and Input-Output (I-O) Industries

Taxable Commodity	I-O Industry Name	I-O Industry Number
Sugar	Sugar	14.19
Petroleum products	Petroleum refining and related products	31.01
Motor vehicles	Motor vehicles and parts	59.03
Tires and tubes	Tires and inner tubes	32.01
Truck and bus bodies	Truck and bus bodies	59.01
Use tax on highways	Truck trailers	59.02
Communications	Communications except radio and television	66.00

Sources: Table compiled by the author. Data from the *Standard Industrial Classification Manual* (Office of Management and Budget, Executive Office of the President, 1972); and the *Input-Output Structure of the U.S. Economy: 1967*, vols. 1, 2, 3 (U.S. Department of Commerce, Office of Business Economics; published as a supplement to the *Survey of Current Business*).

"truck trailers," 80 percent were covered by fewer than ten industries. And in one case, "truck and bus bodies," 90 percent had been covered by the third industry.[6]

The next major step was the establishment of the correspondence between the industries selected by the computer program at the previous step and the retail sales outlets, providing the link between processing activities and final consumption. It was thus necessary first to find a correspondence between the I-O classification and the Standard Industrial Classification (SIC) used in all major statistical sources. Subsequently, one can easily link the I-O industries with the desired statistical series to be used as distributive weights.

In general, the petroleum and auto industries exhibited a high degree of homogeneity; a comparatively small number of weights turned out to be adequate for allocating a large part of total value. "Sugar" was dissimilar with respect to the other industries, but was internally homogeneous, so that one additional weight was sufficient for a large contribution. The most difficult industry was "communications," because it involved many disparate elements, and was also in direct conflict with the petroleum group. In this case a step-by-step marginal decision analysis had to be applied before final convergence was reached. The list of the finally selected weights is given in table 3-3. As described in detail in appendix B, the identification process required two principal methodological stages before arriving at the final scheme (see table 3-4). The finally selected twelve SIC weights achieve in allocating the per-

Table 3-3
List of Weights for the Allocation of Selective Sales Taxes

Standard Industrial Classification	
Code	Title
	Total retail trade
54	Food stores
55	Automotive dealers
56	Apparel and accessories
63	Insurance carriers
65	Real estate
72	Personal services
75	Auto repair
79	Amusement and recreation
80	Medical and other health services
82	Educational services
86	Nonprofit organizations

Source: Selected on the basis of author's computer program. See text and Appendixes A and B for explanation.

Table 3-4
Value of Taxable Industries Covered by Final Set of Weights

Taxable Industry	Percent of Total Value Covered by Set of Final Weights	Percent of Original Set of Weights Covered by Present Subset
Sugar	70	78
Petroleum refining and related products	55	77
Tires and inner tubes	66	89
Truck and bus bodies	93	100
Truck trailers	73	93
Motor vehicles and parts	73	93
Communications except radio and television	59	82

Sources: Table compiled by the author. Data from the *Census of Retail Trade*, 1972 (U.S. Department of Commerce, Social and Economic Statistics Administration, Bureau of the Census); and the *Input-Output Structure of the U.S. Economy:* 1967, vols. 1, 2, 3 (U.S. Department of Commerce, Office of Business Economics; published as a supplement to the *Survey of Current Business*).

centages of total value shown in column 2 of table 3-4. These figures, however, are somewhat misleading, as they present a global picture of the scheme, but do not accurately reflect the contribution of the final set of weights as compared with those of the previous stages. Therefore, column 3 was calculated to indicate the performance of this group *as a proportion of the coverage achieved by the original set.* The performance is shown to be highly satisfactory.

In conclusion, the range of error introduced by the practical imperfections of the present scheme is believed to be substantially less than the inherent limitations of the subjective methodologies that have been used in previous treatments of this and similar problems. The state allocation of tax burdens for excise taxes is presented in table 3-5.

Customs Duties

The regional allocation of customs duties is conceptually analogous to that of selective sales taxes. But it poses many empirical difficulties, because customs are levied on an amazing variety of items at different rates and are not easily amenable to generalized classification.

The methodology is the same as the one developed for excises, and appropriate references will be made in the following text. It must be pointed out that the computational aspects of the allocation were reviewed in the light of the previously selected set of weights for the distribution of tax burdens.

On the basis of (a) the theoretical considerations that dictate the use of an Input-Output (I-O) table, (b), the official Commodity Groupings of Customs, and (c) the availability of the appropriate statistical series, it was established that the optimal operational classification should be as follows:

		Percent of Total Revenues
1.	Miscellaneous manufactured articles	31
2.	Manufactured goods	24
3.	Machinery	13
4.	Food and live animals	9
5.	Transport equipment	7
6.	Fuels and lubricants	4
7.	Chemicals	4
8.	Alcoholic beverages	3
9.	Tobacco products	1
10.	Crude materials	1
11.	Other	3

Of these customs, five are levied on groups of commodities that are used either directly in final consumption, or as unique inputs to the production of well-defined final goods (for example, unmanufactured tobacco); these are "alcoholic beverages," "tobacco products," "food and live animals," "miscellaneous manufactured articles," and "manufactured goods."

"Beverages" and "tobacco" were imputed on the basis of direct data on consumption, and "food and live animals" were allocated by retail sales of Food Stores. The group "miscellaneous manufactured articles" contains, as its name indicates, a variety of items and, together with the group "manufactured goods," it poses certain serious puzzles. The heterogeneity of these categories inevitably entails a loss in accuracy. In principal, one could allocate these groups by several alternative distributive series, but one has to make a decision on the basis of some implied trade-offs. It was finally decided to allocate "miscellaneous manufactured articles" partly by the sales of Apparel Stores (SIC code 56), and partly by the sales of Miscellaneous Shopping Goods Stores (SIC code 594); and to allocate "Manufactured goods" partly by retail sales of Apparel Stores and partly by Total Retail Trade. The analysis that led to the selection of these weights is given in appendix B. Finally, it may be noted that the "other" category is allocated on the basis of Total Retail Trade. In summary, over 70 percent of all customs duties that comprise the category of "final" goods are prorated by a computationally reasonable methodology.

The remaining classes of customs duties are levied on imports that are used to a large extent as inputs in a variety of processing industries. As it was argued in the case of excise taxes, such commodities warrant utilization of existing

Table 3-5
State Allocation of Tax Burden for Excise Taxes, 1972
(in millions of dollars)

	Alcoholic Beverages	Petroleum	Tobacco	Communications	Truck and Bus Bodies	Tires-Tubes	Motor Vehicles	Sugar	Highway Use	Other
Alabama	$61.13	$50.44	$32.49	$19.51	$9.78	$9.33	$6.65	$1.69	$2.29	$23.47
Alaska	14.24	5.33	3.70	1.87	0.66	0.82	0.57	0.20	0.18	2.75
Arizona	46.80	43.66	20.49	16.07	6.43	7.07	5.79	1.18	1.75	16.98
Arkansas	25.96	30.64	17.47	11.26	5.98	5.54	3.70	1.01	1.41	13.95
California	622.47	464.68	216.49	182.82	63.78	77.19	70.86	12.27	17.29	174.29
Colorado	65.19	51.71	27.00	20.09	8.03	8.83	7.49	1.33	2.10	20.92
Connecticut	95.81	66.01	28.24	30.15	8.08	10.59	9.15	1.89	2.26	25.75
Delaware	21.14	12.41	7.66	4.77	1.63	2.00	1.67	0.37	0.44	5.28
District of Columbia	72.29	33.21	53.08	15.05	1.57	3.59	4.95	0.34	0.85	6.41
Florida	263.27	200.01	78.23	77.69	28.08	32.10	26.65	4.62	7.82	70.25
Georgia	117.92	82.99	46.97	32.13	15.07	15.24	12.77	2.37	3.72	37.11
Hawaii	19.23	20.62	5.25	7.64	1.98	3.06	3.42	0.48	0.67	6.65
Idaho	12.59	11.66	7.88	4.40	2.49	2.22	1.40	0.40	0.57	5.92
Illinois	336.97	240.18	116.93	98.08	32.13	38.22	32.15	6.00	8.88	92.40
Indiana	85.04	86.63	68.00	34.08	15.49	15.61	11.43	2.76	3.74	40.88
Iowa	44.50	44.06	26.35	17.54	7.88	7.93	5.79	1.42	1.89	20.95
Kansas	34.56	36.43	21.72	14.05	6.92	6.60	4.52	1.12	1.64	18.99
Kentucky	60.32	48.76	52.78	18.53	8.05	8.43	5.92	1.65	1.96	21.96
Louisiana	69.82	59.58	39.20	23.19	9.54	10.20	7.57	2.10	2.36	25.71
Maine	22.79	16.71	11.66	8.44	2.83	2.97	2.16	0.63	0.68	7.96
Maryland	127.65	84.46	32.64	32.77	11.78	13.74	11.32	2.39	3.20	33.79
Massachusetts	176.76	123.25	57.96	55.00	14.09	19.40	17.12	3.35	4.07	47.40
Michigan	210.47	173.85	100.62	67.11	28.41	30.04	22.83	5.42	7.03	73.54
Minnesota	95.52	68.43	34.22	27.81	9.85	11.44	9.64	1.82	2.59	29.77
Mississippi	37.39	30.38	21.57	11.31	6.10	5.58	3.75	1.10	1.41	14.12
Missouri	99.50	90.03	52.19	36.36	14.19	15.66	13.56	2.45	3.65	36.62

Montana	16.81	11.59	7.13	4.33	2.16	2.08	1.38	0.41	0.50	5.75
Nebraska	35.05	25.36	13.51	10.77	4.08	4.42	3.54	0.71	1.03	11.39
Nevada	40.71	48.25	8.75	23.85	2.05	5.52	3.95	0.38	1.04	5.61
New Hampshire	53.80	17.38	17.82	7.20	2.49	2.89	2.14	0.57	0.64	7.27
New Jersey	221.56	145.82	75.87	57.11	18.46	23.74	21.44	4.55	5.04	60.00
New Mexico	22.40	17.66	8.87	6.53	3.28	3.17	2.31	0.54	0.79	8.20
New York	522.40	454.35	180.97	189.51	38.50	62.25	58.20	10.97	13.29	139.84
North Carolina	102.52	86.59	97.91	33.20	15.27	15.61	12.11	2.66	3.75	37.96
North Dakota	16.42	8.96	5.67	3.53	1.82	1.62	0.96	0.27	0.42	4.54
Ohio	186.74	197.69	111.14	78.14	29.78	33.46	26.92	5.84	7.65	81.59
Oklahoma	45.18	45.05	27.38	16.87	8.40	8.19	6.35	1.38	2.02	19.70
Oregon	44.84	43.04	28.41	16.26	7.36	7.83	6.73	1.39	1.80	18.50
Pennsylvania	217.81	218.69	108.57	89.39	30.48	36.17	30.62	6.52	8.09	89.76
Rhode Island	26.06	18.28	11.40	7.74	2.19	2.88	2.40	0.50	0.61	7.19
South Carolina	72.68	40.26	27.26	15.28	7.16	7.16	5.14	1.38	1.74	18.44
South Dakota	13.88	9.47	5.93	3.72	1.72	1.67	1.13	0.30	0.41	4.89
Tennessee	57.60	67.87	37.50	26.76	12.48	12.46	9.47	2.10	3.01	30.18
Texas	190.93	217.95	106.30	83.80	38.00	38.53	29.90	6.37	9.45	92.08
Utah	13.67	18.85	6.69	7.41	3.42	3.40	2.72	0.54	0.84	8.50
Vermont	19.01	10.63	5.45	4.82	1.31	1.59	0.91	0.30	0.36	3.93
Virginia	106.09	83.73	45.85	31.35	13.64	14.21	10.39	2.55	3.47	35.75
Washington	77.64	65.14	25.77	25.14	9.46	10.89	9.15	2.00	2.46	26.72
West Virginia	29.93	26.62	17.28	9.91	4.33	4.47	2.91	0.91	1.06	11.79
Wisconsin	127.91	74.09	40.82	29.94	11.30	12.33	8.61	2.30	2.86	33.12
Wyoming	9.05	5.52	3.99	2.04	1.05	1.03	0.76	0.18	0.24	2.91
All States	$5,110.00	$4,135.00	$2,207.00	$1,650.00	$591.00	$681.00	$563.00	$116.00	$157.00	$1,637.00

Sources: Table computed by the author. Data from *Annual Statistical Review*, 1972 (Distilled Spirits Institute); *Comparative Cigarette Tax Collections*, 1972 (National Tobacco Tax Association); *Input-Output Structure of the U.S. Economy: 1967*, vols. 1, 2, 3 (U.S. Department of Commerce, Office of Business Economics; published as a supplement to the *Survey of Current Business*); *Census of Retail Trade*, 1972 (U.S. Department of Commerce, Social and Economic Statistics Administration, Bureau of the Census); *County Business Patterns* (U.S. Department of Commerce, Social and Economic Statistics Administration, Bureau of the Census, various years); *Annual Report of the Commissioner of the Internal Revenue Service* (U.S. Department of the Treasury, Internal Revenue Service, 1972 and 1973).

Note: Details may not add to totals due to rounding.

information on the interindustry structure of the economy. Unfortunately, of the five classes included in this general category, only three are allocated on the basis of an I-O table, because it is impossible to find a corresponding industry in the I-O structure for the remaining two. The three groups and the respective industries are given in table 3-6.

The methodology subsequently employed for the determination of the most important industries using these goods as inputs in their economic activities was strictly analogous to that used for excise taxes, and is described in detail in appendix B. The same appendix also contains the reasoning that led to the selection of the final set of weights, which are listed in table 3-7.

As it may be observed by comparing table 3-7 with the list of weights used for excise taxes (table 3-3), there is a net addition of only one weight, namely Miscellaneous Shopping Goods Stores.

There remains the problem of prorating "crude materials" and "machinery." Although these commodities are obviously "intermediate" products, the great diversity of the items involved rules out the use of an I-O table. Consequently, imputation by some kind of final consumption series seems inevitable. Under the assumption that a wide spectrum of retail items is reflected in the composition of "crude materials" and "machinery," Total Retail Trade is used as a basis for their allocation. Such an assumption, although admittedly strong for "machinery," appears perfectly reasonable for "crude materials," as this group contains a sufficiently disparate number of components. The state allocation of burdens for customs duties is presented in table 3-8.

Table 3-6
Correspondence between Dutiable Commodities and Input-Output (I-O) Industries

Dutiable Commodity	I-O Industry Name	I-O Industry Code
Chemicals	Chemicals and selected chemical products	27.00
Transport equipment	Motor vehicles and parts	59.03
Fuels and lubricants	Petroleum refining and related products	31.01

Sources: Table compiled by the author. Data from the *Standard Industrial Classification Manual* (Office of Management and Budget, Executive Office of the President, 1972); and the *Input-Output Structure of the U.S. Economy: 1967*, vols. 1, 2, 3 (U.S. Department of Commerce, Office of Business Economics; published as a supplement to the *Survey of Current Business*).

Table 3-7
List of Weights for the Allocation of Customs Duties

Standard Industrial Classification	
Code	Title
	Retail trade
54	Food stores
56	Apparel and accessory stores
65	Real estate
55	Automotive dealers
63	Insurance carriers
72	Personal services
75	Auto repair
79	Amusement and recreation
80	Medical and other health services
82	Educational services
86	Nonprofit organizations
594	Miscellaneous shopping goods stores

Source: Selected on the basis of author's computer program. See text and Appendixes A and B for explanation.

Table 3-8

State Allocation of Tax Burden for Customs Duties, 1972

(in millions of dollars)

	Miscellaneous Manufactured Articles	Manufactured Goods	Machinery	Food and Animals	Transport Equipment	Fuels and Lubricants	Chemicals	Beverages	Tobacco	Crude Materials	Other
Alabama	$14.18	$11.59	$6.22	$4.20	$2.66	$1.65	$1.52	$1.17	$0.55	$0.58	$1.42
Alaska	1.57	1.19	0.73	0.50	0.23	0.17	0.16	0.27	0.06	0.07	0.17
Arizona	50.11	7.37	4.50	2.93	2.32	1.43	1.51	0.89	0.35	0.42	1.03
Arkansas	7.61	6.78	3.70	2.51	1.48	1.00	0.89	0.50	0.29	0.34	0.84
California	111.54	83.60	46.19	30.38	28.33	15.22	12.35	11.88	3.65	4.30	10.54
Colorado	12.96	9.51	5.54	3.28	3.00	1.69	1.38	1.24	0.46	0.52	1.27
Connecticut	17.39	12.94	6.82	4.68	3.66	2.16	1.93	1.83	0.48	0.63	1.36
Delaware	3.13	2.46	1.40	0.91	0.67	0.41	0.34	0.40	0.13	0.13	0.32
District of Columbia	5.76	3.69	1.70	0.85	1.98	1.09	1.02	1.38	0.89	0.16	0.39
Florida	39.30	32.51	18.62	11.44	10.65	8.55	4.88	5.02	1.32	1.73	4.25
Georgia	21.20	18.01	9.84	5.88	5.10	2.72	2.40	2.25	0.79	0.92	2.24
Hawaii	5.82	3.29	1.76	1.18	1.37	0.68	0.54	0.37	0.09	0.16	0.40
Idaho	2.82	2.52	1.57	0.99	0.56	0.38	0.34	0.24	0.13	0.15	0.38
Illinois	57.66	46.51	24.49	14.85	12.85	7.86	6.67	6.43	1.97	2.28	5.59
Indiana	18.58	18.24	10.83	6.85	4.57	2.84	2.52	1.62	1.15	1.01	2.47
Iowa	10.22	9.61	5.55	3.52	2.31	1.44	1.29	0.85	0.44	0.52	1.27
Kansas	8.92	7.88	4.50	2.77	1.81	1.19	1.04	0.66	0.37	0.42	1.03
Kentucky	10.22	9.95	5.82	4.09	2.37	1.60	1.43	1.15	0.89	0.54	1.33
Louisiana	16.37	12.96	6.81	5.19	3.03	1.95	1.77	1.33	0.66	0.63	1.56
Maine	3.62	3.47	2.11	1.56	0.66	0.55	0.50	0.43	0.20	0.20	0.48
Maryland	19.79	16.24	8.95	5.93	4.53	2.77	2.34	2.44	0.55	0.83	2.04

Massachusetts	33.35	23.84	12.56	8.29	6.84	4.04	3.69	3.37	0.98	1.17	2.87
Michigan	42.61	35.20	19.49	13.44	9.13	5.69	4.93	4.02	1.70	1.81	4.45
Minnesota	14.82	13.47	7.89	4.52	3.86	2.24	1.87	1.82	0.58	0.73	1.80
Mississippi	8.20	7.06	3.74	2.73	1.50	0.99	0.94	0.71	0.36	0.35	0.85
Missouri	17.83	16.78	9.70	6.06	5.42	2.95	2.50	1.90	0.88	0.90	2.20
Montana	3.18	2.71	1.52	1.02	0.55	0.38	0.35	0.32	0.12	0.14	0.35
Nebraska	5.90	5.34	3.02	1.75	1.42	0.83	0.71	0.67	0.23	0.28	0.69
Nevada	4.20	2.79	1.49	0.93	1.58	1.58	0.51	0.78	0.15	0.14	0.34
New Hampshire	4.04	3.24	1.93	1.42	0.86	0.57	0.50	1.03	0.30	0.18	0.44
New Jersey	41.94	20.90	15.90	11.26	8.57	4.77	4.27	4.23	1.28	1.48	3.63
New Mexico	4.62	3.77	2.17	1.34	0.92	0.58	0.50	0.43	0.15	0.20	0.50
New York	112.16	76.19	37.00	27.17	23.27	14.88	12.50	9.97	3.05	3.45	8.44
North Carolina	21.10	18.35	10.06	6.58	4.84	2.84	2.61	1.96	1.65	0.94	2.30
North Dakota	2.46	2.18	1.20	0.66	0.38	0.29	0.27	0.31	0.10	0.11	0.27
Ohio	37.81	36.26	21.62	14.47	10.76	6.47	5.40	3.56	1.87	2.01	4.93
Oklahoma	12.24	10.00	5.22	3.42	2.54	1.48	1.31	0.86	0.46	0.49	1.19
Oregon	9.66	8.21	4.90	3.44	2.69	1.41	1.21	0.86	0.48	0.46	1.12
Pennsylvania	51.48	43.14	23.79	16.16	12.24	7.16	6.33	4.16	1.83	2.22	5.43
Rhode Island	4.77	3.59	1.91	1.24	0.96	0.60	0.52	0.50	0.19	0.18	0.44
South Carolina	9.79	8.84	4.89	3.42	2.06	1.32	1.19	1.39	0.46	0.46	1.12
South Dakota	2.35	2.18	1.24	0.74	0.45	0.31	0.28	0.26	0.10	0.12	0.28
Tennessee	16.31	14.14	8.00	5.21	3.78	2.22	1.98	1.10	0.63	0.74	1.83
Texas	58.83	45.44	24.40	15.78	11.96	7.14	6.23	3.64	1.79	2.27	5.57
Utah	4.99	3.73	2.25	1.34	1.09	0.62	0.54	0.26	0.11	0.21	0.51
Vermont	2.11	1.69	1.04	0.75	0.37	0.35	0.28	0.36	0.09	0.10	0.24
Virginia	18.81	16.70	9.47	6.31	4.16	2.74	2.39	2.02	0.77	0.88	2.16
Washington	14.36	12.15	7.08	4.96	3.66	2.13	1.78	1.48	0.43	0.66	1.62

Table 3-8 (cont.)

	Miscellaneous Manufactured Articles	Manufactured Goods	Machinery	Food and Animals	Transport Equipment	Fuels and Lubricants	Chemicals	Beverages	Tobacco	Crude Materials	Other
West Virginia	5.95	5.57	3.12	2.27	1.16	0.87	0.76	0.57	0.29	0.29	0.71
Wisconsin	16.00	14.68	8.78	5.69	3.44	2.43	2.10	2.44	0.69	0.82	2.00
Wyoming	1.56	1.37	0.77	0.44	0.30	0.18	0.16	0.17	0.07	0.07	0.18
All States	$1,022.20	$789.80	$433.80	$287.30	$225.10	$135.40	$115.40	$97.50	$37.20	$40.40	$99.00

Sources: Table computed by the author. Data from *Annual Statistical Review, 1972* (Distilled Spirits Institute); *Comparative Cigarette Tax Collections, 1972* (National Tobacco Tax Association); *Input-Output Structure of the U.S. Economy: 1967*, vols. 1, 2, 3 (U.S. Department of Commerce, Office of Business Economics; published as a supplement to the *Survey of Current Business*); *Census of Retail Trade, 1972* (U.S. Department of Commerce, Social and Economic Statistics Administration, Bureau of the Census); *County Business Patterns* (U.S. Department of Commerce, Social and Economic Statistics Administration, Bureau of the Census, various years); *Highlights of the U.S. Export and Import Trade* (U.S. Department of Commerce, Social and Economic Statistics Administration, Bureau of the Census, Report FT990, table 13); and *Annual Report of the Commissioner of the Internal Revenue Service* (U.S. Department of the Treasury, Internal Revenue Service, 1972 and 1973).

Note: Details may not add to totals due to rounding.

Notes

1. See, for example, J.A. Pechman, *Federal Tax Policy* (3rd ed.), Studies of Government Finance. Washington, D.C.: The Brookings Institution, 1977, p. 182.

2. The legal definitions of the statutory incidence of these taxes are given in Title 26, Subchapter D, Part 49 of the *Code of Federal Regulations.*

3. H.S. Houthakker and L.D. Taylor, *Consumer Demand in the United States: Analyses and Projections* (2nd and enlarged ed.) Cambridge, Mass.: Harvard University Press, 1970.

4. G.F. Break and J.A. Pechman, *Federal Tax Reform,* Studies of Government Finance. Washington, D.C.: The Brookings Institution, 1975, p. 116.

5. U.S. Department of Commerce, Bureau of Economic Analysis, *Input-Output Structure of the U.S. Economy: 1967,* vols. 1 and 3 (published as a Supplement to the *Survey of Current Business*). For the implementation of the procedure described in the following paragraphs, it is, of course, necessary to assume that the interindustry structure of the U.S. economy remained constant between 1967 and 1972.

6. The details of the computer program, as well as a graphic representation of the sorting procedure, are presented in appendix A.

4

Federal Outlays: Transfer Payments, Grants-in-Aid, and Private Goods

Conceptual Incidence Theory

Overview of Difficulties

As was briefly indicated in the first chapter, the allocation of federal expenditures to the beneficiaries of the associated federal programs is a more complex and precarious task than the allocation of taxes. On a conceptual level the problems are independent of the underlying criterion for distribution—that is, the theoretical difficulties are always present regardless of whether the allocation is attempted by income class, geographical region, or some other criterion. On the empirical level, however, the problems associated with the distribution of federal expenditures among the states in many instances surpass those usually identified with income-size allocations, because, generally speaking, the field of geographical distributions has not been as well plowed by other researchers as has that of income-size distributions. Moreover, the specific statistical information needed for allocation is frequently either unavailable or, at best, inadequate for the methodology dictated by the relevant theoretical considerations.

The complications arising in the expenditure side of the government budget are partly due to the extensive number of federal programs and the objectives for which such programs are designed. Expenditures are more varied than taxes in type, and individual classes of expenditures are more numerous.

Conceptual problems are also generated by the fact that most federal expenditure items fall somewhere in between the "pure private good" and the "pure public good" of economic theory. The notions of "nonexcludability" and of "nonrival" consumption become central to a proper analysis and evaluation of government outlays. But the taxonomy is not always easy; some federal expenditures provide fully excludable benefits to particular individuals, but relatively few provide benefits to "all" residents. Moreover, the distinction becomes fuzzy, since occasionally a "mixed" good may become a "private" good beyond a certain number of consuming units. Such anomalies complicate both the conceptual classification of expenditures and the empirical implementation of a benefit allocation.

But by far the most important limitation in any study that deals with some kind of allocation of government expenditures is the lack of an economic theory of benefit incidence that parallels the theory of tax incidence. As far as "private" or "mixed" goods are concerned, this problem may be—at least, partly—attributed to our limited knowledge about the technical characteristics of the goods or services and of household preferences. As far as "public" goods are concerned, however, the problem in addition reflects the complete absence of the market mechanism, which, in turn, is the *raison d'être* for the public sector itself. To be sure, the absence of a market-determined price for the goods or services that satisfy "social wants" is not *per se* a prohibitive impediment for the development of a theory of benefit incidence, because such a theory may be based on the purely behavioral characteristics of consumers' utility functions. On the other hand, the lack of statistical information on preferences poses severe problems for the empirical implementation of such an approach.

Statement of the Problem

The various influences generated by federal expenditures can be divided into three successive stages of impact. First, the outlays for federal programs generate income in the jurisdictions where payments are made. Second, federal expenditures affect the "welfare" of the beneficiary groups served by the program in question. And third, the expenditure activity of the central government sets in motion economic forces which, over a longer period, may influence not only the welfare but also the behavior of rational economic actors, thus altering the economic environment of decision-making units.

Quite obviously, the latter stage of impact may be analytically examined only within a general-equilibrium framework—a task next to impossible, not only because of the tremendous number of variables involved, but also because the behavioral relationships on which the distribution of personal income is calculated without the federal programs would not be valid under such a drastic change in the institutional setting as is the introduction of the federal budget. To put it differently, the very structure of markets in the absence of government becomes problematic.

In principle, an expenditure analysis comparable to the analysis of the incidence of federal revenues among geographical regions should estimate the incidence of benefits from federal programs accruing to residents in each area. Such a symmetrical analysis of the receipts and outlays sides of the federal budget immediately encounters severe theoretical problems that go beyond the difficulties usually associated with only the tax side. Not the least among these problems is the identification of beneficiary groups, which, for some programs, is difficult even about the initial recipient of the supposed benefit. This is hardly a problem in the tax side, where the *statutory* payer of the tax is always known, but where the manifold aspects of the shifting process change the ultimate bearer of the burden. On the contrary, on the expenditure side, while it is still true that the cases of benefit "snatching" need to be recognized and, if possible, dealt with, it is unfortunately also true that in some instances even the first-order beneficiary of a federal program may not be promptly identifiable. It thus becomes obvious that an analytical investigation of federal expenditures encounters difficulties on many different levels.

Critical Review of the Issues

To put it concisely, the major stumbling block in the allocation of public expenditures is the intricacy of expressing the benefits in income-equivalent terms. This is a direct consequence of the fact that in many cases the market mechanism fails altogether, and in others is, for all practical purposes, inoperative.

Situations in which the market mechanism fails completely are identified in the theory of public finance with the case of "social wants"—that is, those wants that are satisfied by services provided in equal amounts for all. The associated goods are alternatively known as "public," "collective," or "social" goods. The market cannot satisfy such wants, because people cannot be excluded from the benefits and are consequently unwilling to engage in voluntary payments. The principal question here is not only whether there has been a benefit "snatching" from (or perhaps "relinquishing" by) the original recipient, but the more fundamental one, "who is the *initial* beneficiary?" To phrase it in a different way, the problem in this case is not only one of *shifting,* it is also one of *impact.*

Situations in which the market mechanism becomes inoperative (for reasons other than those associated with public goods) are important when there is justification for benefit "snatching" or "relinquishing" that is not reflected in pecuniary terms. For example, who really benefits from food stamp payments to the elderly—the aged themselves or their children who, presumably, are relieved of financial responsibilities? And what about the personal valuation of benefits under the two alternatives? This is, of course, a case parallel to tax incidence where the identification of those who legally are entitled to receive expenditures is easy to determine, but where the question of ultimate incidence may not be lightly assumed away.

If we define as "mixed" goods those goods whose consumption becomes "exhaustive" beyond a certain number of consuming units, we are faced with yet another complication—namely the case of "privatized" public goods, the benefits from which are again difficult to match with a beneficiary group. To be sure, this case is relatively easier than the previous ones, insofar as the two competing candidates are society, on the one hand, and a more or less well-defined subset, on the other. But since there is no theory to explain the degree of "publicness" and how this concept is functionally related to the number of consuming units, any classification is bound to rely on intuitive and to a certain extent arbitrary ideas.

One category of public outlays that, until recently, had not received much attention in the realm of incidence theory is the one comprising the expenditures for the satisfaction of the so-called "merit wants." Merit wants are essentially "private" wants that are satisfied by the market within the limits of effective demand and supply. They become public wants "if considered so meritorious that their satisfaction is provided for through the public budget, over and above what is provided for through the market and paid for by individual buyers."[1] The debate about "merit goods" (that is, goods or services provided through the budget for the satisfaction of "merit wants") had until recently been confined to the philosophical aspects of government interference with individual preferences, the premise of consumer sovereignty, and other similar notions. Recent discussions of merit goods, however, have entered the realm of incidence theory. Specifically, several authors have concluded that in-kind transfers (which are the pragmatic manifestations of "merit goods") are valued by the recipients at less than the dollar amount spent by the government for the corresponding programs.

The point of these investigations is well taken; they claim that what really matters is the personal valuation of these programs by their recipients, not what the government spends for them.[a] We thus return to the basic problem discussed earlier, namely the existence and operational usefulness of utility functions regarding consumers' preferences of public programs. Janice Peskin has given a good account of the problem, by summarizing the views of several researchers about four important types of "merit goods"—food stamps, medicare, medicaid, and public housing.[2] Unfortunately, there is a prohibitive gap between theoretical exercises and empirical reality in this specific area. The results of the studies contained in the Peskin paper are based mostly on subjective utility functions and the simulations on hypothetical households. While few would deny the importance of such theoretical investigations, particularly in terms of the guidelines they provide for future research, it becomes immediately apparent that their applicability to empirical research is severely limited by the hard fact that their conclusions are not directly linked with econometric evidence.[b]

The lack of incidence theory on the expenditure side mainly reflects the vast array of consequences resulting from a given public expenditure. The significance of this observation and its relation to the tax side has been put succinctly by Burkhead and Miner as follows:

[a]These papers view in-kind income solely from the perspective of its direct recipient. They ignore the ramifications related to external benefits.

[b]The procedures employed by these studies point again to the unpleasant dilemma of conceptually correct but practically infeasible procedures, versus empirically operational but theoretically less defensible methodology. For example, one paper uses a utility function but a constant proportion of income spent on food, which results in unreliable estimates. A second study allows for proportions of income spent on food to vary by income level and household size, but does not use utility functions in deriving the estimates! Peskin herself is thus forced to admit that the results are only "gross approximations to cash equivalents."

The relatively direct consequences of public expenditure, [however], go far beyond effects on prices, work efforts, and assets into such diverse influences as those on rate of crime, delinquency, morbidity and mortality, likelihood of nuclear conflict, academic achievement of students, and speed and convenience of communication and transportation. . . . While taxes influence economic and even noneconomic behavior and may influence overall growth and regional economic well-being, they do not in themselves influence the provision of specific services.[3]

The lack of unifying propositions incorporating the necessary theoretical elements on which an analysis of expenditure incidence could be based suggests that a compromise is unavoidable as far as the measurement of fiscal benefits is concerned. Specifically, it appears inevitable to bypass the traditional framework of incidence and, instead, to concentrate on the direct attribution to households of the quantity of services provided. Although this approach may overlook some cases of snatching or relinquishing, it is nevertheless an improvement over the crude methodology that endeavors to determine the direct dollar flows by program. There are, of course, dozens of shifting assumptions that one can think of and actually employ, but since they all derive from heuristic arguments, they are necessarily as creditable as any alternative conjecture. Carl Shoup, who has placed special emphasis on the question of benefit incidence, sums the problem as follows:

The test for whether the benefit from the government service has been relinquished by the initial recipient is a comparison, at a given point in time, between the existing economic condition of the household or firm and the condition it would have been experiencing at the time if the service had not been rendered. Since the second half of this comparison is a description of a hypothetical state of affairs . . . the hypothesis that a relinquishing of the benefit has occurred cannot be tested directly.[4]

Thus the central idea behind the general framework of the present study is the principle of identifying beneficiary groups. In the following section we underline the assumptions and procedures on which our analysis is based.

Assumptions and Procedures

The fundamental assumption of our allocation is that the benefits accruing to individuals stay put with the initial recipient. No external benefits, and no "snatching" or "relinquishing" of benefits are allowed for.

In conjunction with the assumption of nonshiftability, the following operational classification of federal outlays is also employed: (1) direct cash or in-kind income, (2) private goods, and (3) public goods.

The first category corresponds with transfer payments and, by extension, with grants-in-aid; the second, with purchases of goods and services and the surplus or deficit of government enterprises; and the last category is distinct from the others in that it includes total amounts of all types of expenditures for the programs involved.

Transfer Payments. Transfer payments are conceptually equivalent to negative taxes. On the accepted assumption that these outlays do not give rise to external benefits, transfer payments can be allocated to the direct recipients by state.

Transfer payments include in-kind benefits, which have grown in importance sharply since their first initiation. The major federal programs are food stamps, public housing, and medicare. The recently emphasized question of valuation of in-kind transfers opens new avenues for research, but the currently available theoretical results are too limited to be of any practical significance (see p. 58). It is therefore assumed that the costs of the federal programs reflect 100 percent the benefits enjoyed by the recipients.

Private Goods. By "private goods" provided through the federal budget, we mean the purchases of goods and services, as well as the surplus or deficit of government enterprises, the benefits from which accrue to a subset of society that we call the "beneficiary group."

There are obvious problems arising in attempts to convert costs of provision into figures representing benefits to residents of an individual state. Not only are federal programs usually provided directly to the recipients (that is, the market mechanism is bypassed), but such outlays are also known to have many consequences that go beyond the immediate economic effects normally associated with the tax side. With the assumption of no benefit externalities introduced in the beginning of this section, the question of spillovers from one state to another is largely resolved.[c] But there remains the problem of classifying several federal programs as public or private goods. For example, what about Natural Resources or Highways? It is true that the services of these programs accrue to identifiable (at least in principle) individuals. But, with reasonable accuracy, it is also arguable that these outlays should be considered as "social overhead expenditures"—the implication being that they represent, if not indispensable, at least vital prerequisites for the functioning of modern society.

The question is obviously tricky, and the lack of theoretical results regarding the "degree of publicness" renders it subjective conjecture. To retain internal consistency in the methodology of this study, we decided to base the criterion for the classification of federal outlays as "public" or "private" good on the notion of "allocableness" of public expenditures. According to this

[c]This statement is qualified by the adverb 'largely' because the question of which state is the receiving place of benefits may sometimes be independent of spillovers or other externalities. For example, Selma Mushkin ("Distribution of Federal Expenditures," p. 437) wonders: "Is the proper *situs* of the benefits the state in which the retired employee worked, or the state in which he lives in retirement?" Such questions are next to impossible to handle in a large-scale empirical investigation and are consequently ignored in the present study.

yardstick (which, of course, does contain a degree of cyclical reasoning), public goods are expenditures that do not lend themselves to particular individuals or groups.[5] Hence, private goods are those that are subject to specific imputation.

As "private goods" are thus classified all federal expenditures for which a specific beneficiary group could be identified. Accordingly, the following programs are included in this category:

		Percent of Total Outlays
1.	Agriculture	27
2.	Veterans' medical care	12.5
3.	Health and hospitals	12
4.	Social security	12
5.	Housing and urban development	11
6.	Air transportation	8
7.	Other education	4
8.	Labor	4
9.	Veterans' Administration and other services	3
10.	Highways	2
11.	Recreation	2
12.	Higher education	1.5
13.	Elementary and secondary education	1

The specific incidence assumption pertaining to each program is specified in the sequel along with the method of allocation.

Public Goods. Public goods occupy a central position in the theory of public finance. The idiosyncracies associated with their production and distribution have stimulated nothing less than some of the most celebrated contributions to the history of the field. It therefore comes as no surprise that in the realm of fiscal incidence they also have enjoyed the lion's share of original research. But there has actually been little progress as far as operational results are concerned, and even less uniformity in the opinions of the experts. As a result, investigations of the incidence of public expenditures normally use alternative methodologies for the allocation of benefits derived from public goods.

In the present monograph, the allocation of public goods embodies an attempt to recognize and address two problems: First, the classification of the pertinent programs, which is based on distinguishing between *final* and *intermediate* public goods; and second, the methodology of distribution, which is linked with consumer preference indicators in a way consistent with the treatment of taxation. (A complete analysis of the public goods question is the topic of the next chapter.)

In summary, federal expenditures are classified for the purposes of this study as follows:

1. Public goods (all types of outlays): $124,698 million, or 52 percent of total expenditures.
2. Transfer payments: $61,645 million, or 26 percent of total expenditures[d] (this figure excludes the programs classified as public goods).
3. Grants-in-aid: $32,264 million, or 14 percent of total outlays[d] (this figure again excludes programs regarded as public goods).
4. Private goods (consisting of the corresponding goods and services and surplus of government enterprises): $19,008 million or 8 percent of total federal expenditures.

Table 4-1 illustrates schematically the above methodology for the functional classification used by the *Survey of Current Business.*

Estimation of Benefit Distribution by State

The actual total allocated figure is $237.093 billion. The discrepancy between this figure and the amount reported in table 4-1 is due to the different totals for transfer payments and for grants-in-aid. Since the data for these programs were obtained from direct sources of the Census Bureau it was deemed expedient to retain the "control totals" of these sources, because their figures were regarded more reliable than those in the *Survey of Current Business.* Thus transfer payments are $62.041 billion (or $396 million more than the figure reported in the *Survey of Current Business*), and grants-in-aid are $31.346 billion (or $918 million less).

Allocation of Transfer Payments and Grants-in-Aid

According to the analysis in the preceding section, transfer payments are allocated directly to the recipients by state of residence. Grants-in-aid are also allocated directly. They have been left out of the previous discussion because they are the clearest instance of federal outlays on behalf of the states.

Transfer payments are the sum of eight federal programs by state: (1) Old Age, Survivors, and Disability Insurance, (2) Railroad benefits, (3) Black Lung benefits, (4) Unemployment Insurance programs, (5) Federal Medicare, (6) Veterans Readjustment, (7) Educational Assistance—wives and widows of veterans, and (8) Food Stamps.

Grants-in-aid are the sum of the following seven items: (1) Education,

---

[d]The actual allocated amounts differ slightly from these figures. See following section.

(2) Employment Security Administration, (3) Health and Hospitals, (4) Highways, (5) Housing, (6) Public Welfare, (7) all other.

The figure for each program reflects the sum of the amount provided directly to state governments plus the amounts provided to local governments, which were subsequently grouped by state. Note that from the allocation of both transfers and grants have been excluded the amounts corresponding to the programs that have been classified as public goods. Table 4-2 presents figures of this allocation.

Allocation of Private Goods

According to the analysis in the first section of this chapter, "purchases of goods and services" and "surplus or deficit of government enterprises" for the "private" goods produced by the Federal Government are to be distributed to the direct beneficiaries of such outlays. The specific assumptions and method of allocation follow.

Elementary and Secondary Education. Benefits are assumed to accrue to the families of students enrolled in elementary and secondary education schools. Since all federal funds go to public schools, allocation is performed by enrollment in public schools by state. Total amount allocated is $153 million.

Higher Education. Benefits are assumed to accrue to the families of students enrolled in institutions of higher education. Of the total $206 million, 45 percent or $92.7 million are contributed to public institutions, and 55 percent or $113.3 million to private institutions. Therefore, allocation is achieved by the corresponding figures for enrollment in private and public colleges and universities in 1972. In addition, the enrollment figures are corrected for the interstate migration of students, so that benefits are attributed, as is conceptually desirable, to the residence of the student rather than to the state where he or she studies.

Other Education. This category includes occupational, vocational, and adult education, education for the handicapped, public libraries, and other items. Benefits are assumed to accrue either to individuals who participate directly in one of the programs listed previously, or to the residents of a state at large. Allocation follows a similar breakdown by state for federal funds obligated by the Office of Education for fiscal year 1972. Total allocated figure is $731 million.

Health and Hospitals. Benefits are assumed to accrue to patients in federally funded hospitals during the year 1972. Allocation by state is performed on the basis of the average daily census of patients. Total figure is $2.339 billion.

Table 4-1

Functional Classification of Federal Expenditures, 1972

(in millions of dollars)

	Public Goods				
	Goods and Services	*Government Enterprises*	*Transfers and Interest*	*Grants*	*Total*
National Defense	$74,751	$−117	$10,046	$505	$85,185
Space Research	3,289			62	3,351
International Affairs	749	11	2,750	5	3,515
General Government	6,721	−144	21,724	284	28,585
Sanitation	71		9	673	753
Police and Correction	130			343	473
Natural Resources	2,895	−383	12	312	2,836
Subtotal	*88,606*	*−633*	*34,541*	*2,184*	*124,698*

	Private Goods				
	Goods and Services	*Government Enterprises*	**Transfer Payments**	**Grants in Aid**	**Total**
Elementary and Secondary Education	$153		$662	$2,524	$4,639
Higher Education	203	$3	327	1,094	1,878
Other Education	731			820	1,878
Health and Hospitals	2,339		1,009	1,359	4,707
Social Security	2,300	4	55,551	15,801	73,656
Labor	753		555	2,701	4,009
Veterans Education and Insurance			3,492		3,492
Veterans Medical Care	2,352			23	2,375

Veterans Administration	571	6		3	580
Highways	195	129		4,649	4,973
Air Transportation	1,504	67		160	1,731
Urban Renewal	950		44	2,321	3,315
Public Housing	1,006	177			1,183
Agriculture	551	4,627	4	702	5,884
Recreation	387		1	107	495
Subtotal	*13,995*	*5,013*	*61,645*	*32,264*	*112,917*
Total					**237,615**

Source: Table rearranged and compiled by the author. Original data from the *Survey of Current Business* (U.S. Department of Commerce, Office of Business Economics, July 1974; *Census of Government–Governmental Finances*, 1972 (U.S. Department of Commerce, Bureau of the Census, Magnetic tape).

Table 4-2

State Allocation of Transfer Payments and Grants-in-Aid, 1972

(in millions of dollars)

	Transfer Payments	*Grants-in-Aid*
Alabama	$926.06	$602.79
Alaska	55.39	179.63
Arizona	546.16	261.99
Arkansas	585.60	319.17
California	6,704.38	4,145.89
Colorado	605.85	414.01
Connecticut	1,046.36	371.18
Delaware	142.85	93.27
District of Columbia	330.98	506.01
Florida	2,802.16	754.35
Georgia	1,037.21	721.36
Hawaii	190.47	190.76
Idaho	192.51	125.53
Illinois	3,392.27	1,850.89
Indiana	1,341.85	486.75
Iowa	882.58	302.31
Kansas	690.86	287.38
Kentucky	984.69	491.67
Louisiana	1,081.57	572.73
Maine	326.36	174.12
Maryland	979.73	500.80
Massachusetts	1,993.72	914.35
Michigan	2,686.20	1,306.94
Minnesota	1,197.09	588.68
Mississippi	572.99	400.70
Missouri	1,505.27	618.39
Montana	199.62	168.45
Nebraska	431.21	177.75
Nevada	118.30	92.13
New Hampshire	201.98	86.92
New Jersey	2,350.03	906.82
New Mexico	264.95	265.97
New York	6,517.09	3,359.32
North Carolina	1,152.36	629.67
North Dakota	189.59	111.98
Ohio	2,961.91	1,023.62
Oklahoma	729.19	449.15
Oregon	547.87	418.59

Table 4-2 (cont.)

	Transfer Payments	Grants-in-Aid
Pennsylvania	4,170.45	1,452.68
Rhode Island	346.24	150.68
South Carolina	595.77	325.37
South Dakota	186.68	113.55
Tennessee	1,153.02	552.38
Texas	2,718.01	1,443.71
Utah	254.26	224.76
Vermont	143.24	102.24
Virginia	1,039.93	584.22
Washington	890.94	560.33
West Virginia	686.63	349.90
Wisconsin	1,304.01	517.26
Wyoming	86.72	96.65
All States	$62,041.00	$31,346.00

Sources: Transfer payments compiled by the author. Grants in aid compiled by Mr. James Trask. Original data from *Census of Governments–Governmental Finances*, 1972 (U.S. Department of Commerce, Bureau of the Census, Files A and B, Magnetic tape); and from unpublished sources (U.S. Department of Commerce, Bureau of Economic Analysis, Social and Economic Statistics Administration. Data for 1972 made available directly to the author).

Note: Details may not add to totals due to rounding.

Social Security. Benefits are assumed to be enjoyed by recipients of social security payments. Allocation is therefore carried out on the basis of social security transfer payments and, in particular, of the component "civilian programs." Total allocated figure is $2.304 billion.

Labor. Similarly, benefits from the purchases of goods and services of this program are assumed to go hand in hand with grants-in-aid. Allocation therefore follows the distribution of Employment Security Administration grants. Total figure is $753 million.

Veterans' Medical Care. Benefits are assumed to accrue to the direct recipients of medical services. The distribution by state follows the pattern of fiscal year 1972 as presented in the *Annual Report of the Administrator of Veterans' Affairs*. Total figure is $2.352 billion.

Veterans' Administration and Other Services. Similarly, the benefits from this federal program are allocated by state by means of the reported distribution for fiscal 1972. Total figure is $577 million.

Table 4-3

State Allocation of Private Goods Benefits, 1972

(in millions of dollars)

	Agriculture	Veterans Medical Care	Health and Hospitals	Social Security	Housing and Urban Development	Air Transportation	Other Education
Alabama	$94.89	$48.03	$48.46	$35.53	$34.48	$1.70	$15.14
Alaska	0.25	1.98	13.74	2.06	15.48	11.99	2.58
Arizona	36.57	26.39	34.07	21.61	8.31	20.69	7.84
Arkansas	146.04	37.21	49.13	23.72	21.88	3.13	7.95
California	351.39	244.11	270.36	215.49	184.61	99.94	56.76
Colorado	74.13	28.88	42.11	20.59	21.63	4.25	11.87
Connecticut	10.38	29.30	20.96	35.73	50.68	31.29	10.39
Delaware	14.08	7.95	8.15	5.70	0.10	2.17	2.97
District of Columbia	0.12	72.66	56.94	6.37	98.49	74.68	10.38
Florida	132.21	79.32	85.14	113.60	39.64	200.39	23.27
Georgia	127.51	48.62	78.04	40.79	51.36	33.83	18.93
Hawaii	7.41	2.59	16.63	6.03	13.24	20.62	1.59
Idaho	52.14	4.73	4.58	8.12	1.17	11.10	4.16
Illinois	283.93	126.18	111.27	125.29	112.22	136.59	31.00
Indiana	139.62	38.91	22.30	58.98	27.48	44.42	18.65
Iowa	413.42	38.25	15.14	35.85	11.10	7.28	10.49
Kansas	262.43	35.81	30.98	26.98	35.22	27.81	10.41
Kentucky	128.50	31.13	50.87	35.40	34.37	1.44	13.89
Louisiana	96.37	36.91	48.29	32.95	21.79	22.90	14.78
Maine	16.31	12.83	21.26	12.74	3.84	49.55	4.44
Maryland	31.88	32.51	47.64	34.92	32.16	18.22	5.06
Massachusetts	8.90	81.00	41.04	69.47	114.82	99.70	19.09
Michigan	91.43	64.80	35.09	99.87	78.71	35.00	29.07

Minnesota	224.38	47.61	18.54	41.96	57.18	15.21	13.21
Mississippi	132.70	27.41	42.81	21.72	6.16	2.56	10.35
Missouri	185.58	57.40	58.49	58.59	33.34	39.76	15.29
Montana	100.33	6.48	7.70	7.94	2.60	0.38	4.28
Nebraska	226.36	22.86	23.34	17.98	3.10	4.37	6.87
Nevada	9.14	5.14	6.07	4.59	2.02	12.34	2.66
New Hampshire	4.20	5.30	6.49	9.45	4.97	9.12	3.59
New Jersey	9.14	46.27	37.08	86.52	86.11	39.89	21.77
New Mexico	34.10	14.15	21.43	8.98	18.88	0.30	7.63
New York	64.00	222.25	175.15	233.70	327.80	110.80	54.52
North Carolina	185.33	53.36	57.22	47.94	31.80	1.32	21.67
North Dakota	135.17	6.27	7.47	6.83	0.40	2.39	4.79
Ohio	120.10	94.66	51.83	116.40	75.31	5.98	31.52
Oklahoma	106.51	26.74	27.50	30.28	21.17	4.53	9.50
Oregon	53.13	28.06	11.83	27.49	28.78	0.28	10.07
Pennsylvania	67.71	116.29	119.50	149.79	164.31	140.24	37.40
Rhode Island	1.48	10.90	12.98	12.07	22.01	0.89	4.03
South Carolina	50.91	21.35	43.29	23.37	18.46	4.72	11.92
South Dakota	141.10	18.74	16.88	7.93	4.17	0.03	4.74
Tennessee	81.05	63.32	49.47	40.76	60.17	3.39	16.01
Texas	345.22	114.32	178.12	105.55	64.49	55.92	43.08
Utah	19.52	15.95	11.49	9.36	0.17	8.87	6.57
Vermont	14.58	5.69	3.99	5.33	1.95	18.01	3.38
Virginia	58.32	54.09	97.31	41.59	41.21	19.45	17.14
Washington	112.93	42.59	45.31	38.88	18.03	36.64	13.54
West Virginia	4.70	29.56	28.68	24.26	10.79	13.87	7.47
Wisconsin	146.79	54.86	22.34	54.34	12.14	61.77	15.42
Wyoming	23.48	10.25	4.44	3.43	1.18	0.05	2.48
All States	$5,178.00	$2,352.00	$2,339.00	$2,304.00	$2,133.00	$1,571.00	$731.00

Table 4-3 (cont.)

	Labor	Veterans Administration	Highways	Recreation	Private Higher Education	Public Higher Education	Elementary and Secondary Education
Alabama	$11.45	$8.01	$5.76	$0.88	$0.94	$1.33	$2.67
Alaska	3.42	0.91	0.53	37.72	0.07	0.13	0.29
Arizona	10.81	5.78	3.66	29.13	0.13	1.45	1.65
Arkansas	7.15	5.15	3.69	2.66	0.54	0.59	1.57
California	71.88	47.02	31.56	35.20	9.09	17.21	15.31
Colorado	5.17	7.43	4.09	20.66	0.41	1.28	1.95
Connecticut	13.23	4.46	4.18	0.00	2.68	1.07	2.26
Delaware	2.04	1.49	0.90	0.02	0.10	0.24	0.45
District of Columbia	2.40	112.52	0.76	0.01	0.87	0.22	0.47
Florida	11.96	17.80	12.41	2.73	2.25	2.90	5.15
Georgia	16.68	11.10	8.77	1.79	1.26	1.43	3.71
Hawaii	3.14	2.01	0.83	0.21	0.24	0.45	0.62
Idaho	5.36	2.27	1.46	29.61	0.32	0.35	0.63
Illinois	35.61	30.66	15.95	0.40	8.21	4.85	7.99
Indiana	11.08	7.46	9.16	0.25	2.16	1.79	4.15
Iowa	8.30	4.85	5.43	0.13	1.66	0.88	2.20
Kansas	8.23	5.31	4.39	0.21	0.57	1.18	1.61
Kentucky	8.13	5.96	5.24	0.69	0.98	1.06	2.43
Louisiana	13.02	7.33	5.40	0.87	1.01	1.57	2.88
Maine	5.76	3.32	1.64	0.10	0.25	0.31	0.85
Maryland	12.44	4.86	5.54	0.11	1.86	1.71	3.13
Massachusetts	25.47	10.89	7.13	0.06	8.72	1.86	4.09

Michigan	37.59	13.26	14.21	2.83	3.06	4.68	7.47
Minnesota	10.58	19.04	6.56	2.80	1.47	1.68	3.09
Mississippi	7.25	5.69	3.88	1.31	0.58	0.93	1.79
Missouri	19.02	11.06	8.54	1.41	2.29	1.69	3.50
Montana	3.85	2.32	1.50	25.41	0.18	0.38	0.60
Nebraska	3.76	3.23	2.90	0.43	0.49	0.66	1.12
Nevada	5.01	1.66	1.22	53.54	0.03	0.20	0.44
New Hampshire	2.41	1.80	1.20	0.61	0.28	0.17	0.57
New Jersey	32.09	9.80	10.15	0.06	4.54	2.37	5.15
New Mexico	3.40	3.52	2.22	23.39	0.18	0.55	0.97
New York	94.48	26.86	18.61	0.12	21.74	7.34	11.99
North Carolina	10.68	8.39	8.80	1.82	2.25	1.77	3.95
North Dakota	4.64	1.92	1.34	1.62	0.05	0.34	0.48
Ohio	32.61	16.64	16.00	0.16	5.17	3.78	8.24
Oklahoma	10.85	7.51	5.40	0.80	1.12	1.31	2.07
Oregon	15.76	5.07	3.92	27.40	0.59	1.41	1.60
Pennsylvania	43.01	38.94	16.32	0.48	10.04	3.40	8.03
Rhode Island	5.65	2.70	1.19	0.00	0.84	0.35	0.64
South Carolina	6.87	5.91	4.55	0.70	1.44	0.80	2.12
South Dakota	3.01	2.01	1.49	2.72	0.28	0.28	0.55
Tennessee	9.89	7.75	6.83	1.12	1.42	1.35	3.03
Texas	27.46	38.56	22.42	2.02	5.33	5.54	9.31
Utah	9.64	3.05	1.99	31.56	0.93	0.63	1.04
Vermont	3.43	1.45	0.72	0.21	0.17	0.13	0.36
Virginia	10.78	7.12	7.68	1.77	1.38	1.78	3.63
Washington	23.53	8.52	5.19	10.15	1.21	2.24	2.69
West Virginia	6.11	4.20	2.43	0.83	0.39	0.60	1.40

Table 4-3 (cont.)

	Labor	Veterans Administration	Highways	Recreation	Private Higher Education	Public Higher Education	Elementary and Secondary Education
Wisconsin	14.13	7.18	6.81	1.54	1.50	2.28	3.38
Wyoming	2.69	1.26	0.99	26.71	0.00	0.20	0.29
All States	$753.00	$577.00	$324.00	$387.00	$113.30	$92.70	$153.00

Sources: Table computed by the author. Original data from the *Survey of Current Business* (U.S. Department of Commerce, Office of Business Economics, various issues); *Statistical Abstract of the United States* (U.S. Department of Commerce, 1973 and 1975); *Residence and Migration of College Students* (U.S. Department of Health, Education, and Welfare, National Center for Educational Statistics, 1970); *Digest of Educational Statistics* (U.S. Department of Health, Education, and Welfare, 1973); *Hospitals: A County and Metropolitan Area Data Book* (U.S. Department of Health, Education, and Welfare, 1972); unpublished data (U.S. Department of Commerce, Bureau of Economic Analysis); *Census of Governments–Governmental Finances*, 1972 (U.S. Department of Commerce, Bureau of the Census, Files A and B, Magnetic tape); *Annual Report of the Administrator of Veterans' Affairs*, 1973; *Highway Statistics* (U.S. Department of Transportation, Federal Highway Administration, 1972); *Commuter Air Carrier Traffic Statistics, Year Ended December 1972* (Federal Aviation Administration, Civil Aeronautics Board); and *Selected Outdoor Recreation Statistics* (U.S. Department of the Interior, Bureau of Outdoor Recreation, 1972).

Note: Details may not add to totals due to rounding.

Highways. Benefits are assumed to be enjoyed by private users. This is indeed an assumption necessitated by practical considerations. In principle, a distinction should be made between private and commercial users; the benefit derived by the latter could perhaps be subsequently assumed as being relinquished to consumers. Unfortunately, since there is no available information on interstate commodity traffic, this sort of separation turns out to be empirically impossible. The allocative series used is total motor fuel consumption by state. Total distributed figure is $324 million.

Air Transportation. Benefits are assumed to accrue to consumers of air travel. The allocation of this federal expenditure by state is based on figures of air traffic in passenger-miles for 1972. Total allocated figure is $1.571 billion.

Housing and Urban Development. Benefits are assumed to accrue to the direct recipients of public housing and to the residents of the area where urban renewal programs are undertaken. The definitional problems associated with these two categories were severe, due to the startling inconsistencies in the figures given in the *Survey of Current Business* and in other governmental publications. It is our understanding that, irrespective of the taxonomy followed by individual agencies, the amounts associated with these federal programs are essentially "grants" to state and local governments. Consequently, the allocation is achieved by means of the state distribution of grants for this program. Total figure is $2.133 billion.

Agriculture. Federal expenditures in this area are used almost entirely for price support programs. Therefore, benefits are assumed to be enjoyed by farm proprietors. The allocative series is the distribution of farm income by state for 1972. Total allocated figure is $5.178 billion.

Recreation. Benefits are assumed to accrue to the users of federally owned recreation areas. In principle, the statistical series should include information on visitor-days. But as such data are not available, allocation is achieved on the basis of acreage, under the assumption that visitor-days are proportional to the available area. Total allocated figure is $387 million.

The results of the allocation of benefits from all private goods by state for 1972 are presented in table 4-3.

Notes

1. Musgrave, *Theory of Public Finance*, p. 13.
2. Janice Peskin, *In-Kind Income and the Measurement of Poverty*, tech-

nical paper VII, U.S. Department of Health, Education, and Welfare, October 1976.

3. Jesse Burkhead and Jerry Miner, *Public Expenditure*, Chicago: Aldine Publishing Company, 1971, p. 325.

4. Carl Shoup, *Public Finance*, Chicago: Aldine Publishing Company, 1969, p. 89. The futility of rigorous endeavors in this area is illustrated again by the fact that, after a conscientious effort to discuss as many aspects of this problem as possible, Professor Shoup finally comes up with only hypothetical examples in support of his ideas propounded in the preceding analysis.

5. See also Musgrave, Case, Leonard, "Distribution of Fiscal Burdens," p. 281.

5 Federal Outlays: Public Goods

Conceptual Incidence Theory

The most intractable problem in the area of expenditure incidence is the imputation of benefits from public goods. The problem of allocation is usually preceded by two additional questions: first, which public expenditures to classify as "public goods"; and second, which public goods are to be regarded as final products rather than intermediate products or inputs. The latter distinction normally implies different rules of allocation.

In the present monograph, the question of classification is resolved by the method of elimination—that is, by classifying as "public goods" those federal outlays that are not amenable to specific imputation to a well-defined beneficiary group. This reasoning is not really as crude as it might seem at first sight. It is in the nature of public goods to be "unallocable" insofar as the benefits derived from their production and distribution cannot be traced to any particular subset of society. From the point of view of incidence theory, the single most important characteristic of public goods is that their value to society at large transcends the specific benefits that may accrue to individuals. Transfer payments of the Department of Defense, for example, are regarded as more valuable to society than to the individual recipients. And more generally, the activities of that department are not designed to benefit members of the armed forces—instead, their purpose is to protect the lives and property of the people of all states of the Union.

Complications arise, however, upon realizing that this is not a sharp distinction. The classification of a federal expenditure as a a public good does not rule out the presence of some "private" component. Consider, for instance, the case of highways. While there is no question that a particular set of consumers (that is, users of highways) derive direct utility from federal outlays, it is also obvious that the importance of the highway system may be traced down to manifold ramifications of the American way of life. Should not, then, federal highway expenditures be allocated as a "public good"? Not surprisingly, there is no unique answer to this and similar questions. The theory of fiscal incidence does not provide a measure of "publicness" of the goods and services made available through the budget. And although for the most important public goods there has never been a serious problem of taxonomy, there are still some items for which classification is largely based on intuitive grounds.

In view of these difficulties, it was considered more important to achieve

75

consistency in the treatment of all federal outlays rather than to pursue the will-o'-the-wisp of measurement of the elusive "index of publicness." Therefore, as explained in chapter 4, the classification of government expenditures as "private" or "public goods" is conducted by the method of elimination: all federal outlays that cannot be apportioned to well-defined beneficiary groups are regarded as "public goods." Accordingly, the following expenditures are regarded as "public goods" in this study:

1. National defense
2. Space research
3. International affairs
4. General government
5. Sanitation
6. Police and Correction
7. Natural resources

The next immediate question to be resolved is which of these government "purchases" or "transfers" are to be regarded as final products, and which as intermediate products or "costs" for the provision of other final goods. As in the case of private markets where certain consumer outlays are only instrumental, some government purchases are not directly sources of utility themselves but are necessary inputs to activities that may yield utility. The importance of this distinction—at least for the purposes of the present investigation—lies in the implications concerning the apportionment of benefits: public goods entering final consumption are to be geographically imputed by means of a general methodology (discussed in the next section). Those identified as intermediate products, however, are to be allocated in accordance with the geographical distribution of the final outlays which they "support."

A clear analysis of these issues—although in a different context—has been presented by W. Nordhaus and J. Tobin in their paper "Is Growth Obsolete?"[1] In this paper, a pioneering attempt to substitute a measure of "true" economic welfare for the traditional output measures of the national accounts, the authors conclude that very little government expenditure on goods and services can be considered consumption. In their view, most public outlays are either "intermediate inputs" (such as General Government and Sanitation) or "regrettables" (such as National Defense and International Affairs). Referring to defense expenditures, for example, the authors remark "No reasonable country (or household) buys national defense for its own sake. If there were no war or risk of war, there would be no need for defense expenditures and no one would be the worse without them."[2]

Within the framework of the Nordhaus-Tobin paper, the line between final and instrumental outlays is not hard to draw. The authors focus on consumption as the index of *economic* welfare and consequently exclude all items that add to neither actual nor sustainable household consumption. But in general the issue is too controversial to be resolved decidedly one way or another.

In the present study we do not feel as strongly about the argument that national defense expenditures are "regrettables." We also have similar reservations about Space Research and International Affairs. Benefits under an all-embracing definition may result from federal activities that yield not only economic consumption but also "consumption" of such intangibles as freedom, prestige, and power. The philosophical problems raised by these concepts are of course too deep to be resolved in the realm of fiscal incidence. Nevertheless, in our judgment the associated federal programs could also be regarded as final goods that increase the welfare of households directly. In our opinion, only expenditures for general government and for natural resources may be classified as clear-cut intermediate products or inputs. These expenditures do not yield direct utility to households but represent the necessary social overhead costs of a complex industrial state. They are instrumental outlays that provide the infrastructure for the continuance of society.

All the same, the presence of many conceptual difficulties and philosophical worries cannot justify an inflexible attitude on these matters. We therefore decided to present two alternative allocations of public goods. The first variant is based essentially on the Tobin-Nordhaus conclusions and assumes that all government "purchases" or "transfers" classified above as "public goods" are in effect intermediate inputs for the production of "private goods," which were treated in the previous chapter. Consequently, public goods are allocated according to the geographical distribution of private goods.

The second variant assumes that only General Government and Natural Resources are intermediate inputs to be allocated as in the first variant. National Defense, Space Research, International Affairs, Sanitation, and Police and Correction are regarded as final expenditures and are imputed by a general methodology, the many aspects of which are described in the following section.

The Use of Preference Indicators

The most frustrating aspect of the allocation of public goods is the derivation of a general methodology that will best impute the benefits among the citizens of the country—whether they are grouped by income class, residence, profession, or any other analytically useful criterion.[a] Geoffrey Brennan describes succinctly the complexities of this undertaking in the following words:

Traditionally, the way this problem has been handled seems to have involved the setting out of a number of alternative allocations (equal sum per family, benefits

---

[a]This section deals exclusively with final public goods. For convenience the adjective "final" is therefore omitted in the ensuing discussion.

proportional to income, and so on) in the hope that the end result might turn out to be not too sensitive to this dimension of the total calculation—a hope which, almost invariably, proves unfounded.[3]

If direct preferences for public goods are unobservable, differences in utilities derived from the consumption of a public good may be depicted only in terms of a clear quantitative component that is obedient to normal conventions of economic analysis. By far the single most important index of the level of an individual's economic welfare has been income, and policy measures affecting the income distribution of population have long been regarded as the best available instruments for influencing the direct economic satisfactions of households. Thus if the benefits from public goods can be successfully translated into some "income-equivalent" terms, we simultaneously obtain both the best available index of utility and a pecuniary quantity that may serve as the basis for interpersonal comparisons.

But the definition of "income" in this kind of endeavour plays a crucial role whose significance cannot be overemphasized. First, the standard formulation of preference indicators as a relationship between utility and quantities of goods consumed is valid as an index of welfare only if, given the same prices faced by all, an individual with twice the income of another consumes exactly twice as much good as the other. Second, if an individual's consumption pattern does not conform to the principle just outlined, then, according to Samuelson's analysis of revealed preference, it must be the case that by reallocating expenditure from the initial bundle of goods the consumer has been able to secure extra consumer surplus.

These considerations pose severe limitations for the empirical utilization of "income-equivalent" measures as indexes of utility, unless certain restrictions are imposed on the interpretation of the key concepts. In particular, if a consumer, given the doubling of his income, could have bought twice as much of a good, but did not do so, it must be assumed that the resulting consumer surplus (in "income-equivalent" terms) has been directly proportional to his income; and that the same proportion governs the relationship of any other consumer with his own surplus. More important, greater income may be taken to imply greater welfare only if a rise in income entails increases in consumption of all goods. This normally does not happen, *unless income is defined as quantities times the marginal rates of substitution.*

This definition of income, although still inadequate for expressing "true" welfare valuations by, and changes among individuals, represents a conceptual improvement for the allocation of benefits from public goods over the traditional heuristic methodologies.

Consider figure 5-1: the horizontal axis depicts the amount of public goods, and the vertical the amount of private goods that are regarded as equivalent to private income. Suppose that the preferences of an individual between private

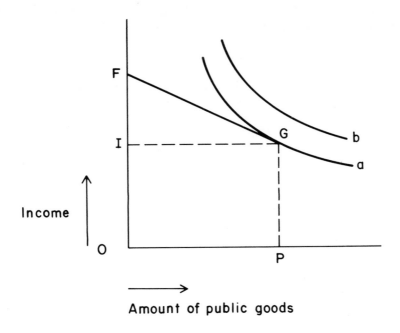

Figure 5-1. Diagrammatic Representation of Benefits Valuation

and public goods are known and are reflected by indifference curves such as *a* and *b*. Furthermore, suppose that this individual earns private income of 0*I* and consumers 0*P* units of public goods. 0*I* and 0*P* are coordinates of a point *G* on the individual's preference map, which lies on indifference curve *a*. If a tangent is now drawn at point *G* on indifference curve *a*, it will intersect the ordinate at *F*. The amount *FI* is the value of 0*P* units of public goods expressed in terms of private income. This may be seen by recalling that the slope of *FG* is the marginal rate of substitution between public goods and income; if income is taken as the numeraire, the marginal rate of substitution may be thought of as the subjective value or price to the individual of a unit of public goods. Thus *FI* is the value of 0*P* units of public goods measured in terms of private income.

This is the core proposition contained in two articles by Henry Aaron and Martin McGuire, who endeavored to illustrate that the allocation of public goods benefits must be linked with the theory of consumer preference, if only because of the sound conceptual foundations that are embodied in this theory.[4] Since the methodology of the present study derives from the Aaron-McGuire analysis, their model will be presented first. Subsequently, we discuss the extensions and modifications on which our procedures are established.

The Aaron-McGuire Model. For a typical individual—for example a—Aaron-McGuire postulate the following utility function:

$$U_a = f(Y_a, P) = f_1(Y_a) + f_2(P) \tag{5.1}$$

where Y_a is the value of commodities consumed by individual a alone (regarded as equivalent to private income), and P is the total quantity of public goods which, by definition, are common to all individuals. The key assumption reflected in equation (5.1) is that utilities of private goods and of public goods are independent. As will be argued later, this is too strong an assumption.

The marginal rate of substitution of public goods for income is then given by

$$MRS_{Y_a,P} \equiv \frac{\partial U_a/\partial P}{\partial U_a/\partial Y_a} = \frac{MU_a(P)}{MU_a(Y)} \tag{5.2}$$

We then have for any individual j:

$$YP_j = MRS_{Y_jP} \times P \tag{5.3}$$

In words, YP_j is the value to individual j of P units of public goods measured in terms of income. This follows from the usual first-order conditions of utility maximization by taking income as the "numeraire" and multiplying the quantity of public good with its "subjective value" or "price."

Consider two individuals a and b. It is true that

$$YP_a = MRS_{Y_aP} \times P \tag{5.4}$$

and

$$YP_b = MRS_{Y_bP} \times P \tag{5.5}$$

Substituting equation (5.2) into (5.4) and an analogous expression into equation (5.5), and dividing equation (5.4) by equation (5.5), we obtain:

$$\frac{YP_a}{YP_b} = \frac{MU_a(P)/MU_a(Y)}{MU_b(P)/MU_b(Y)} \tag{5.6}$$

Assume, now, that all individuals, including a and b, have identical preference maps. Since their preference indicators have been assumed to be separable in public and private goods, the marginal utility that both a and b derive from public goods will be equal, namely

$$MU_a(P) = MU_b(P) \qquad (5.7)$$

Using equation (5.7) to simplify equation (5.6) we have:

$$\frac{YP_a}{YP_b} = \frac{MU_b(Y)}{MU_a(Y)}$$

and, in general,

$$\frac{YP_i}{YP_j} = \frac{MU_j(Y)}{MU_i(Y)} \qquad (5.8)$$

for all i and j.

Equation (5.8) is Aaron's and McGuire's central proposition: It states that the imputed benefits from public goods should be allocated to individuals in inverse proportion to their marginal utilities of income. For determining the proportions YP_i/YP_j etc., only the ratios of the *MRS*'s matter; therefore $MU_i(P) = MU_j(P)$ arbitrarily may be set equal to k so that equations (5.3) and (5.8) now yield:

$$YP_i = \frac{k}{MU_i(Y)} \times P \qquad (5.9)$$

By assumption, utilities of private goods and of public goods are independent. Therefore, the marginal utility of income in equation (5.9) is a function of income only, and may consequently be evaluated.

Extensions to the Aaron-McGuire Model. Granted its assumptions, the model of Aaron and McGuire constitutes a general framework from which specific allocation rules can be deduced depending upon the value of the elasticity of marginal utility of income. These results have been derived in appendix C. The main conclusions are as follows. Let θ be the elasticity of marginal utility of income.

If $\theta = 0$, benefits from public goods are allocated equally on a per-capita basis. This implies that incidence is progressive, in the sense that the poor benefit more than the rich.

If $\theta = -1$, allocation is proportional to income. Hence, incidence, too, follows a "proportional" pattern.

If $\theta < -1$, benefits are allocated in proportion to income raised to the power θ. Consequently, the resulting pattern of incidence is regressive, in the sense that the richer the individual, the more benefits he receives from government expenditures on public goods.

The assumption that preferences for private and public goods are independent is certainly crucial for the development of the Aaron and McGuire model. The authors discuss it briefly in their second paper but conclude that "On balance, the assumption of independence *does not seem unreasonable*" (emphasis theirs).[5] There is little doubt that the hypothesis of separability of preferences is a simplifying assumption that helps tremendously the empirical implementation of the whole scheme. On the other hand, it also obscures the plausible supposition that the marginal utility of public goods is affected by income. It is therefore interesting to see how the conclusions of Aaron and McGuire are likely to be modified if the assumption of separability is relaxed.

In this case benefits from public goods—expressed in income-equivalent terms—are given by the following equation:

$$YP = \frac{\partial U/\partial P}{\partial U/\partial Y} \times P \tag{5.10}$$

where symbols are defined as they were earlier.

To determine how the imputation of benefits varies with income, we differentiate equation (5.10) with respect to income:

$$\partial YP/\partial Y = \frac{(\partial^2 U/\partial Y \partial P)(\partial U/\partial Y) - (\partial U/\partial P)(\partial^2 U/\partial Y^2)}{(\partial U/\partial Y)^2} \times P \tag{5.11}$$

The sign of the derivative is determined by the numerator, in which, following the conventional assumptions about the functional form of utility indicators, $\partial U/\partial Y > 0$, $\partial U/\partial P > 0$ and $\partial^2 U/\partial Y^2 \leqslant 0$. If $\partial^2 U/\partial Y^2 = 0$, the derivative is zero, because $\partial^2 U/\partial Y \partial P$ is also equal to zero. This is the case of constant marginal utility of income which implies separable preferences for private and public goods. Constant marginal utility is a sufficient but not a necessary condition for the derivative to vanish.

If $\partial^2 U/\partial Y^2 < 0$, the sign of equation (5.11) is determined by the relative magnitudes of the numerator in conjunction with the sign of $\partial^2 U/\partial Y \partial P$: this is the term (missing from the Aaron-McGuire formulation) that indicates how the marginal utility of public goods is affected by private income. We postulate that this derivative is negative—that is, the utility of public goods declines with income. This proposition is not only a plausible hypothesis (police protection means less to the person who has a private guard than to the person who doesn't), but also a direct consequence of the substitutability between the two goods as presumed by the form of the utility function. In the usually employed forms of preference indicators the term to the left of the minus sign in the numerator of equation (5.11) outweighs the term to the right. Therefore, $\partial YP/\partial Y$ is generally negative, indicating a "progressive" incidence pattern of public goods.

Consider, for example, the *generalized* form of the two utility functions employed in the Aaron-McGuire paper:

$$U = ln\,(Y^c + P^d) \qquad (5.12)$$

and

$$U = A - \frac{B}{Y^c + P^d} \qquad (5.13)$$

where A,B are arbitrary constants, and c,d are parameters. The permissible values of the parameters of both functions[b] are $c,d > 0$. It can then be shown that

$$\partial YP/\partial Y \lessgtr 0 \ \text{ according as } \begin{cases} c > 1 \\ c = 1 \\ 1 > c > 0 \end{cases}$$

The most important conclusion of this generalized formulation is that income distribution would never deteriorate by the introduction of public goods. The allocation rule implied by both equations (5.12) and (5.13) is expressed by

$$YP_i = \frac{Y_i^{1-c}}{\sum_i Y_i^{1-c}} \times P \qquad (5.14)$$

where YP_i is the value of public goods to individual i, Y_i is his private income, and P is the total value of available public goods. It is immediately obvious that, given the permissible values of c, the most "regressive" allocation of public goods will result from a valuation procedure based on $Y_i^{1-\epsilon}$, where ϵ is arbitrarily small. Therefore, even allocation proportional to income (which preserves the original income distribution) may be only asymptotically reached. For the remaining values of c, imputation is performed either on a per-capita basis, or inversely proportional to a power of income.

It is worthwhile to point out at this juncture that in the generalized, nonseparable form of utility functions, parameter c cannot be interpreted as the elasticity of marginal utility of income—a concept that played an important part in the Aaron-McGuire model. Technically speaking, c is the absolute value of the inverse of the elasticity of substitution but, alas, little insight is added by this interpretation.

What have we gained from the introduction of the term that describes how

---

[b]The restriction is imposed by the requirement that marginal utilities be positive.

the utility of public goods is affected by private income? Basically, a more realistic evaluation of benefits as interpreted by different income classes. Assuming that the marginal utility of public goods is the same for all individuals (the Aaron-McGuire model) means that the evaluation of public goods is ultimately influenced only by the economic status of those involved. Allowing for the utility to be influenced by private income (our extension) means that the *substitutability* between private and public goods has also bearing on the evaluation.

Although the recent empirical investigations assume separability more or less for reasons of convenience (Shlomo Maital calls it a "necessary evil"),[6] the conceptual problem seems to have existed in the literature for quite some time. Discussing how the benefits from a public garden should be apportioned to various income groups, Erik Lindahl wrote: "The subjective utility of the garden may be taken to be roughly the same for all; but utility in terms of money is much higher for the rich than for the poor."[7] It is clear from this passage that Lindahl implicitly assumed a separable utility function: the subjective utility is roughly the same only if the particular want is satisfied exclusively by a public good. In this case, of course, the price that a rich man is willing to pay depends upon his income alone. Otherwise (that is, if the rich man has satisfied his want by a substitute private good), it is doubtful that he would be disposed to pay the same price as before.

Benefit Imputation by State

The theoretical analysis of the previous section provides a link between several well-known empirical techniques with propositions embodied in the economic analysis of consumer preferences and of pure public goods. It is a general methodology whose specific realization depends upon the functional form of the postulated preference indicator.

But as is frequently the case in economic research, the empirical implementation of this approach is not an easy task. As equation (5.10) suggests, the practical application of this procedure requires information on the marginal rate of substitution between private and public goods—a concept that is usually unknown and perhaps unmeasurable.

Things are considerably simplified, however, if one employs the convenient assumption of an additively separable utility function because, as equation (5.9) indicates, informational requirements are then reduced to measuring only the elasticity of marginal utility of income. Armed with three identical and independent estimates of this crucial parameter, Shlomo Maital computes net fiscal incidence for the United States and concludes that much of the progressivity on the tax side is nullified by regressively distributed benefits from public goods.[8]

Maital's attempt is an exemplary blend of theory and measurement, but his results are less than surprising, given that the estimate of the elasticity was −1.5. As explained in detail in appendix C, if the absolute value of this parameter is greater than 1, a regressive pattern of benefit distribution necessarily results.

The most important caveat to this approach concerns the extent of biases introduced by the assumption of separability. We believe that the Aaron-McGuire model in general, and Maital's application in particular, *understate* the degree of rich-to-poor redistribution in the calculation of net fiscal incidence. Specifically, we presume that many final public goods may be substituted for by private goods as one ascends the income ladder. There are goods for which direct substitution can be made (such as police protection and sanitation), and goods whose value is reduced because individuals have ways to hedge by private means against the eventuality that expresses the *raison d'être* of the public good (such as national defense).

Since the "true" form of utility indicators is unknown, it appears best to adopt a procedure that keeps a balance between the two extremes, namely between exaggerating and understanding the redistributive effects of final public goods. We have thus decided to assume the existence of a utility function that implies per capita apportionment of benefits. For example, both utility functions employed by Aaron and McGuire for expository purposes imply per-capita allocation if generalized to nonseparable formulations [equations (5.12) and (5.13) with $c = d = 1$]. It is also important to recall that we have equated total expenditure benefits to total provision costs. Since the cost of providing a given quantity of social goods is constant for all households, a distribution proportional to the number of individuals accurately reflects the "costs incurred on behalf of" the general public.

In this study we present two variants of the geographical distribution of public goods. Variant 1 assumes that all public goods expenditures are to be interpreted as intermediate goods in the production of federal private goods and allocated in accordance with the geographical distribution of the latter. Total allocated figure is $124.698 billion.

Variant 2 assumes that General Government and Natural Resources are the only intermediate inputs to be allocated as in the first variant. They comprise $31.421 billion or 25 percent of total public goods expenditures for 1972. The remaining federal programs are regarded as final expenditures that enter directly the utility of individuals and are apportioned on a per-capita basis. They represent 75 percent of total public goods outlays or $93.277 billion.

The results of the allocation under the two variants are set forth in table 5-1.

Table 5-1
State Imputation of Public Goods Benefits, 1972
(in millions of dollars)

	Variant 1[a]	Variant 2[b]
Alabama	$2,039.28	$2,091.08
Alaska	362.13	236.82
Arizona	1,127.44	1,163.41
Arkansas	1,348.22	1,239.21
California	13,868.55	12,637.68
Colorado	1,402.74	1,412.32
Connecticut	1,813.00	1,836.53
Delaware	313.43	334.75
District of Columbia	1,413.33	692.97
Florida	4,754.40	4,489.10
Georgia	2,443.50	2,735.87
Hawaii	506.87	493.25
Idaho	492.65	462.34
Illinois	6,960.04	6,790.54
Indiana	2,457.51	2,987.11
Iowa	1,930.35	1,778.30
Kansas	1,585.88	1,415.55
Kentucky	1,993.13	1,983.14
Louisiana	2,174.99	2,222.49
Maine	703.08	636.75
Maryland	1,900.07	2,292.08
Massachusetts	3,772.55	3,546.92
Michigan	5,003.95	5,298.27
Minnesota	2,495.30	2,365.47
Mississippi	1,374.46	1,356.91
Missouri	2,906.41	2,858.82
Montana	590.29	469.47
Nebraska	1,027.91	943.48
Nevada	348.95	326.68
New Hampshire	376.17	441.50
New Jersey	4,047.11	4,311.78
New Mexico	744.06	669.48
New York	12,476.81	11,371.39
North Carolina	2,461.20	2,958.92
North Dakota	527.33	416.87
Ohio	5,063.55	6,078.85
Oklahoma	1,590.58	1,580.25
Oregon	1,311.25	1,309.17

Table 5-1 (cont.)

	Variant 1[a]	Variant 2[b]
Pennsylvania	7,254.34	7,160.79
Rhode Island	635.33	594.15
South Carolina	1,239.91	1,516.53
South Dakota	559.38	445.56
Tennessee	2,275.50	2,397.44
Texas	5,746.23	6,645.96
Utah	665.46	672.52
Vermont	338.26	291.29
Virginia	2,204.95	2,690.09
Washington	2,011.18	2,037.86
West Virginia	1,300.12	1,131.67
Wisconsin	2,469.42	2,649.67
Wyoming	289.40	227.92
All States	$124,698.00	$124,698.00

Sources: Table computed by the author. Data from tables 4-1, 4-2, 4-3, and the *Statistical Abstract of the United States* (U.S. Department of Commerce, 1973, 1974 and 1975).

Note: Details may not add to totals due to rounding.

[a]Under the first variant, all public goods are allocated in accordance with the distribution of federal private goods. See text.

[b]Under the second variant, 25 percent of public goods are allocated in accordance with the distribution of federal private goods; 75 percent are imputed on a "per-capita" basis. See text.

Notes

1. W. Nordhaus, and J. Tobin, "Is Growth Obsolete?" in *Economic Growth,* Fiftieth Anniversary Colloquium V. New York: National Bureau of Economic Research, 1972.

2. Ibid., p. 7.

3. G. Brennan, "The Distributional Implications of Public Goods," *Econometrica* 44 (March 1976):391.

4. H. Aaron, and M. McGuire, "Efficiency and Equity in the Optimal Supply of a Public Good," *Review of Economics and Statistics* (February 1969); and "Public Goods and Income Distribution," *Econometrica* 38 (November 1970).

5. Ibid., p. 5.

6. Shlomo Maital, "Public Goods and Income Distribution: Some Further Results," *Econometrica* 41 (May 1973): 563.

7. Referred to by Maital, ibid., p. 567.

8. Shlomo Maital, "Apportionment of Public Goods Benefits to Individuals," *Public Finance/Finances Publiques*, no. 3, 1975.

6

Net Fiscal Incidence: Findings and Conclusions

We have now examined the incidence of the total tax structure and the effect of all public expenditures for 1972. It remains only to determine the net fiscal incidence—that is, the change in the economic position of the residents of a state due to both the tax and expenditure policies of the public sector. Before turning to that task, however, it would be useful to examine the evidence pertaining to the five alternative allocations of the corporate income tax and to consider the conclusions that might have some bearing on the interpretation of net fiscal incidence.

The Importance of the Alternative Allocations of the Corporate Income Tax

As was pointed out in chapter 2, the conflicting theoretical results regarding the incidence of the corporate income tax necessitated the utilization of four alternative hypotheses for the geographical distribution of this tax.

More specifically, the four alternative assumptions regarding the shifting and incidence of the tax were the following: (1) full forward shifting = incidence on consumers; (2) no shifting = incidence on owners of corporate capital; (3) shifting to the rest of capital = incidence on owners of capital at large; and (4) full backward shifting = incidence on labor. The last hypothesis could not be readily implemented because of lack of statistical information on corporate sector payrolls. Therefore, two alternative distributive series were utilized: (i) manufacturing payroll, and (ii) total payroll. (For a discussion of the many involved aspects of the incidence of the corporate income tax, refer to chapter 2.)

The question naturally arises concerning how "different" the five alternative distributions are. Does the controversy regarding the incidence of the tax have any significance when viewed from a geographical standpoint?

The question may be given two interpretations: first, how "similar" or "dissimilar" are the allocations in a statistical sense; and second, how important are their differences by some quantitative index? It is possible for two statistical series to be "dissimilar," yet for their quantitative differences to appear unimportant within a specific framework. Interpretation is, of course, a subjective matter. In general, the importance of this distinction lies in the differential nature of the questions that may be addressed. Roughly speaking, an index of "similarity" is significant in an analytical sense, whereas a quantitative index of differences carries weight in terms of predictive ability. Both of these criteria were employed in the case of the corporate income tax to draw some conclusions about the differential tax burden of the five alternative allocations.

To answer the question of quantitative differences, a simple regression equation was estimated for the five cases using each and every hypothesis as the dependent variable and, in turn, each of the remaining four as the independent variable, as follows:

$$CIT(i) = c + b\ CIT(j),\ i,j = I, \ldots , V;\ i \neq j \tag{6.1}$$

where $CIT(i)$ is the allocation of the corporate income tax burden based on the ith incidence assumption. In total, twenty simple regressions were calculated covering the whole spectrum of linear relations among the five incidence assumptions.

The relationship between a given pair of allocations did *not* imply any causality in the usual econometric sense. Rather, the question to which such a regression addresses itself is this: suppose that the "true" (but unknown) incidence assumption is reflected in allocation i, and that, instead, allocation j has been used. How important is the resulting difference?

The standard error of regression provides a measure of the predictive ability of the equation. For any given incidence assumption, therefore, the standard error indicates the expected deviation in predictions of the per-capita level of the corporate tax burden when estimated by an alternative hypothesis.

Table 6-1 presents the standard errors for the five groups of equations that "explain" a particular incidence assumption with the remaining four alternative hypotheses. The association has been estimated on a per-capita basis.

Using the standard error as a criterion for quantitative differences does not lead to very surprising conclusions. The average amounts of per-capita tax burden for the five alternative assumptions are, respectively, $154 for the first, $136 for the second, $170 for the third, $124 for the fourth, and $137 for the fifth. Compared with these averages, the standard errors under all of the five groups are too large to affirm any equivalence between two alternative hypotheses in quantitative terms. For example, the *lowest* standard errors in each of these groups expressed as a percentage of the corresponding average tax burden ranged from a minimum of 9 percent (under incidence I) to a maximum of 65 percent (under incidence III). Obviously, it does not appear permissible to ignore the quantitative variations in the differential impact of the alternative incidence assumptions.

The alternative criterion of "similarity" was subsequently applied to all possible pairs of incidence hypotheses. Similarity is judged on the basis of the regression coefficient and the constant term between a pair of regressions in which the roles of the dependent and the independent variable have been

Table 6-1
Standard Errors of Regression
(in dollars per person)

	Regressions	
"True" Hypothesis	*Explanatory Hypothesis*	*Standard Errors*
I	II	$13.31
I	III	15.94
I	IV	16.13
I	V	14.32
II	I	56.18
II	III	66.99
II	IV	60.82
II	V	48.31
III	I	114.37
III	II	113.85
III	IV	113.50
III	V	111.27
IV	I	64.01
IV	II	57.17
IV	III	62.78
IV	V	51.64
V	I	33.18
V	II	26.50
V	III	35.91
V	IV	30.13

Sources: Table estimated and compiled by the author. Data from table 2-2 and the *Statistical Abstract of the United States* (U.S. Department of Commerce, 1973, 1974 and 1975).

Incidence Assumptions
  I = On Consumers
  II = On Owners of Corporate Capital
  III = On Owners of Capital at Large
  IV = On Labor (manufacturing payroll)
  V = On Labor (total payroll)

reversed. The hypotheses that the constant term is not statistically different from zero and that the regression coefficient is not statistically different from one are tested at the 1 percent level of significance. The outcomes of the tests are shown in table 6-2; Roman numerals represent the assumption about incidence, as shown in table 6-1. Data are again per capita.

Interpreted literally, the outcome of the tests suggests that no statistical

Table 6-2
Statistical Inference about the Regression Coefficient (b) and the Constant Term (c)

Regressants[a]	Regressors[a]				
	I	*II*	*III*	*IV*	*V*
I		$c \neq 0$ $b \neq 1$	$c \neq 0$ $b \neq 1$	$c \neq 0$ $b \neq 1$	$c \neq 0$ $b \neq 1$
II	$c \neq 0$ $b \neq 1$		$c \neq 0$ $b \neq 1$	$c \neq 0$ $b \neq 1$	$c = 0$ $b = 1$
III	$c \neq 0$ $b = 1$	$c \neq 0$ $b \neq 1$		$c \neq 0$ $b \neq 1$	$c \neq 0$ $b \neq 1$
IV	$c = 0$ $b = 1$	$c \neq 0$ $b \neq 1$	$c \neq 0$ $b \neq 1$		$c = 0$ $b = 1$
V	$c = 0$ $b = 1$	$c \neq 0$ $b \neq 1$	$c \neq 0$ $b \neq 1$	$c \neq 0$ $b \neq 1$	

Sources: Table estimated and compiled by the author. Data from table 2-2 and the *Statistical Abstract of the United States* (U.S. Department of Commerce, 1973, 1974 and 1975).

[a]The notation is set forth in table 6-1.

equivalence has been found between any two conflicting assumptions with regard to the incidence of the corporate income tax. Whereas in some cases the constant term was statistically equal to zero and the regression coefficient statistically equal to one, these results did not obtain when the roles of the regressor and the regressant were reversed.

In conclusion, it does not appear possible to ignore the practical importance of the controversy that characterizes the incidence of the corporate income tax. Allowing for the statistical and informational problems that have possibly affected the accuracy of the estimates, the picture is nevertheless quite clear: from a geographical viewpoint, too, the burden of the corporate income tax is distributed differentially depending upon the specific hypothesis about shifting. That the question remains unsettled in a regional dimension as well implies that more econometric research is necessary before any hypothesis can be confirmed.

Net Fiscal Incidence: Findings and Implications

It is useful to recapitulate at this point the purpose of this study. Our principal objective has been to estimate burdens and benefits in a manner that, given the unavoidable empirical constraints, will best reflect the "true" valuation of taxes and expenditures by households. This objective dictates that expenditures be attributed independently from taxes to successfully assess the simultaneous activity of the central government and its influence on the distribution of income. If this happens, the imputed benefits from public goods may be interpreted as the sum that a taxpayer would be willing to pay as a price for the benefit he receives. These hypothetical payments, however, generally differ from his actual tax payments, and the resulting differential (including the direct benefits from federal private goods) represents the notion of net fiscal incidence.

Major Features of Net Fiscal Incidence

The geographical distribution of net fiscal transfers among the fifty states for 1972 is set forth in table 6-3.[a] There are five estimates of the tax burden, corresponding to the five alternative allocations of the corporate income tax; and there are two estimates of expenditure benefits, corresponding to the two variants in the imputation of public goods. Thus there are in total ten alternative estimates of *net fiscal benefits,* which are defined as *total expenditure benefits less total tax burdens.* Figures are per capita and have been rounded off to the nearest dollar.

The major features of the pattern of net fiscal incidence under all allocations may be summarized as follows. Of the fifty states, sixteen have negative per-capita net benefits for at least one version of the distributional methodology. Of these, six (Florida, Iowa, Nebraska, New York, North Carolina, and Virginia) exhibit both positive and negative benefits, depending on the particular combination of incidence assumptions. With the exception of Virginia, the frequency of negative instances for these states is very low—three times in the case of North Carolina, twice for Nebraska and New York, and once for Florida and Iowa. Since the number of variations is low and, in addition, the dollar amounts are small, the statistical margin of error as a cause of this discrepancy cannot be ruled out. In the case of Virginia there is an equal number of positive and negative net benefits. Here the determining factor is the incidence assumption of public goods, because the change in sign occurs *between* the two variants only.

Eight of the remaining states invariably have a negative pattern of net benefits, and two (Indiana and Michigan) show negative benefits under all but one incidence assumption. Table 6-4 illustrates their rankings according to the alternative allocations presented in this study.

[a]The District of Columbia has been omitted from the analysis in this section because its special statutory nature has resulted in many complications. The alternative would have been to work out many *ad hoc* adjustments, but this solution was finally regarded to be undesirable.

Table 6-3
Per-Capita Net Fiscal Incidence by State, 1972

(in dollars)

	Incidence Assumptions[a]									
	1.I	1.II	1.III	1.IV	1.V	2.I	2.II	2.III	2.IV	2.V
Alabama	$353	$422	$402	$360	$376	$368	$437	$416	$375	$391
Alaska	805	938	884	937	854	414	547	492	545	462
Arizona	69	97	125	155	103	88	116	144	173	122
Arkansas	587	632	581	620	631	532	577	526	565	575
California	204	198	233	232	206	142	137	172	170	145
Colorado	81	132	72	157	112	85	136	76	161	116
Connecticut	−199	−330	−207	−267	−227	−192	−322	−200	−260	−220
Delaware	−238	−424	−226	−314	−254	−200	−386	−188	−276	−217
Florida	107	8	138	228	164	70	−29	101	191	127
Georgia	46	103	104	69	62	109	166	167	132	125
Hawaii	44	43	79	160	64	27	26	62	143	37
Idaho	435	529	361	506	491	394	488	320	465	450
Illinois	−15	−37	−68	−64	−49	−30	−52	−83	−79	−64
Indiana	−131	−81	−131	−217	−145	−31	19	−31	−117	−45
Iowa	376	433	19	391	402	322	379	−35	337	348
Kansas	456	489	238	510	496	380	413	162	434	420
Kentucky	356	397	357	368	377	353	394	354	365	374
Louisiana	347	397	383	406	369	360	410	396	419	382
Maine	517	479	549	544	558	451	413	483	478	492
Maryland	−252	−247	−207	−198	−222	−153	−148	−108	−100	−123
Massachusetts	154	115	189	134	132	114	75	149	94	92
Michigan	−61	−53	−19	−165	−86	−28	−20	14	−132	−53
Minnesota	282	323	222	296	286	248	289	188	262	252
Mississippi	505	565	535	528	541	497	557	527	520	534
Missouri	174	176	136	171	167	164	166	126	161	157
Montana	734	806	632	842	803	563	635	461	671	632
Nebraska	346	392	−76	410	379	290	336	−132	354	323
Nevada	−206	−146	−74	−27	−177	−248	−188	−116	−69	−216
New Hampshire	−192	−193	−138	−164	−144	−106	−107	−52	−78	−58
New Jersey	−180	−237	−174	−220	−196	−143	−200	−137	−183	−159
New Mexico	548	596	619	668	604	477	525	548	598	533
New York	104	16	96	84	50	44	−44	36	24	−10
North Carolina	−14	18	−4	−43	9	80	112	91	52	104
North Dakota	868	952	402	988	934	691	775	225	813	757
Ohio	−127	−117	−104	−211	−153	−32	−22	−10	−116	−58
Oklahoma	315	379	316	384	352	311	375	312	380	348
Oregon	110	164	117	143	138	109	163	116	142	137

Table 6-3 (cont.)

	Incidence Assumptions[a]									
	1.I	1.II	1.III	1.IV	1.V	2.I	2.II	2.III	2.IV	2.V
Pennsylvania	135	106	149	84	116	127	98	141	76	108
Rhode Island	254	196	289	230	250	211	153	246	187	207
South Carolina	58	121	104	34	75	163	226	209	138	180
South Dakota	880	967	674	981	945	710	797	504	814	875
Tennessee	180	241	231	416	192	210	271	261	201	222
Texas	0	41	17	54	23	78	119	95	132	101
Utah	312	374	379	387	350	318	384	385	393	356
Vermont	447	435	509	489	487	343	331	405	385	382
Virginia	−101	−88	−54	−63	−74	0	13	48	40	28
Washington	121	165	88	156	142	129	177	96	164	150
West Virginia	582	605	622	595	584	487	510	527	500	489
Wisconsin	80	113	57	33	76	120	153	97	74	116
Wyoming	640	669	640	775	706	459	488	459	595	525

Sources: Table computed by the author. Data from tables 2-1, 2-2, 3-5, 3-8, 4-2, 4-3, 5-1, and the *Statistical Abstract of the United States* (U.S. Department of Commerce, 1973, 1974 and 1975).

Note: The District of Columbia has been omitted from this table. See text note a, p. 93.

[a]Incidence assumptions are represented by Arabic numerals 1 and 2, which refer to the two variants of public goods allocation, and by Roman numerals I to V, which refer to the five alternative allocations of the corporate income tax. See tables 5-1 and 6-1 for details.

There are no pronounced differences, one way or another, between the two variants of the public goods allocation. Variations do occur according to the alternative incidence assumptions of the corporate income tax, but no state appears to fare consistently better or worse under one public goods variant relative to the other. One can single out Delaware as the overall top state, because it holds the first position under six, and the second under the remaining four allocations. Connecticut roughly ranks second, and New Jersey third.[b]

Of these ten states with negative per-capita benefits, eight rank within the top fourteen states in terms of per-capita personal income. Only Indiana ranks twentieth and New Hampshire thirtieth in that respect. Moreover, as inspection of table 6-4 reveals, five of those states lie in the northeast, and four in the Great Lakes region. The only outlier is Nevada.

At the other extreme, table 6-5 presents the ranking of the ten top states with highest per-capita net benefits under all incidence assumptions. Compared to the rankings of table 6-4, the two variants of public goods produce different,

[b]The reader should perhaps be reminded that table 6-4 refers to algebraic rankings. For example, Delaware is the state that benefits *the least* from the fiscal activity of the central government.

Table 6-4
Ranking of States with Negative Per-Capita Benefits According to Alternative Incidence Assumptions

(rank order, from highest to lowest)

	Incidence Assumptions[a]									
	1.I	*1.II*	*1.III*	*1.IV*	*1.V*	*2.I*	*2.II*	*2.III*	*2.IV*	*2.V*
Connecticut	4	2	2	2	2	3	2	1	2	1
Delaware	2	1	1	1	1	2	1	2	1	2
Illinois	10	10	9	9	9	9	7	6	8	6
Indiana[b]	7	8	6	4	7	8	...	8	5	10
Maryland	1	3	3	6	3	4	5	5	7	5
Michigan[b]	9	9	10	7	10	10	9	...	4	9
Nevada	3	6	8	10	5	1	4	4	10	3
New Hampshire	5	5	5	8	8	6	6	7	9	7
New Jersey	6	4	4	3	4	5	3	3	3	4
Ohio	8	7	7	5	6	7	.8	9	6	8

Source: Table compiled by the author on the basis of table 6-3.
[a]The notation is set forth in table 6-3.
[b]Indiana and Michigan have positive net benefits under assumptions 2.II and 2.III, respectively.

Table 6-5
Ranking of Ten Top States with Positive Per-Capita Net Benefits According to Alternative Incidence Assumptions

(rank order, from highest to lowest)

	Incidence Assumptions[a]									
	1.I	*1.II*	*1.III*	*1.IV*	*1.V*	*2.I*	*2.II*	*2.III*	*2.IV*	*2.V*
Alaska	3	3	2	3	3	10	6	6	7	10
Arkansas	6	6	7	7	6	4	4	4	6	4
Maine	9	10	8	9	9	9	10	7	10	8
Mississippi	10	9	9	10	10	5	5	3	8	5
Montana	4	4	4	4	4	3	3	8	3	3
New Mexico	8	8	6	6	7	7	7	1	4	6
North Dakota	2	2	10	1	2	2	2	10	2	2
South Dakota	1	1	1	2	1	1	1	5	1	1
West Virginia	7	7	5	8	8	6	8	2	9	9
Wyoming	5	5	3	5	5	8	9	9	5	7

Source: Table compiled by the author on the basis of table 6-3.
Note: The District of Columbia has been omitted from this table. See page 93, n. a.
[a]The notation is set forth in table 6-3.

if not markedly so, results for the top ten states. The first variant results in a more homogeneous ordering than the second: with only two exceptions (assumption 1.III for both North Dakota and West Virginia), the ranks of all states are not separated by more than two places. On the other hand, the second variant exhibits a more diverse pattern.

This finding turns out to be characteristic of the net benefit distribution as a whole. The *Spearman* rank correlation coefficient was estimated for all pairs of corporate tax incidence under the first and second variants of public goods. The results are presented in table 6-6.[c]

The results indicate that there is a greater cohesion under the first than under the second variant of public goods, since the correlation coefficients of the former are greater than or equal to those of the latter for every single comparison. The interpretation is obvious: the second variant of public goods is potentially a more effective hypothesis of income redistribution than is its first counterpart. This conclusion is indeed confirmed later (see table 6-9).

It is impossible to find a meaningful taxonomy of the top ten states with highest net benefits in terms of per-capita personal income. On the other hand, they can be easily classified geographically: they lie either in the Rocky Mountains or in the southern part of the country. The only exceptions are Alaska and Maine.

In general, one major conclusion may be drawn from this analysis: there is a clear pattern of net fiscal transfer from the more industrialized parts of the country—the East Coast and the Great Lakes—to the South and the Rocky Mountains. In this respect, the spatial activity of the federal government may be termed "progressive."

Federal Fiscal Transfers and the State
Distribution of Income

Evaluating the importance of the ten alternative incidence assumptions is a difficult task, because the rank permutations of the states do not constitute *per se* a useful criterion. If the ten different patterns of fiscal transfers are to be meaningfully compared, it is necessary to apply a robust procedure that can, in principle, provide unambiguous answers under all circumstances. Accordingly, the importance of the alternative allocations is reckoned by choosing for each

---

[c]Despite the fact that a ranking is a less accurate way of expressing an ordered relation, a nonparametric statistic, such as Spearman's rank correlation coefficient, is, in our opinion, to be preferred to a parametric test. Whereas a simple correlation coefficient would have no value as a test statistic unless the binomial distribution were known or assumed, Spearman's rank correlation coefficient affords a test whose model does not specify conditions about the parameters of the population from which the sample was drawn.

Table 6-6

Spearman Rank Correlation Coefficients between Alternative Net Benefit Allocations

Public Goods Variant 1		Public Goods Variant 2	
Incidence Assumptions[a]	*Correlation Coefficient*	*Incidence Assumptions*[a]	*Correlation Coefficient*
1.I with 1.II	0.98	2.I with 2.II	0.98
1.I with 1.III	0.92	2.I with 2.III	0.88
1.I with 1.IV	0.97	2.I with 2.IV	0.96
1.I with 1.V	0.99	2.I with 2.V	0.98
1.II with 1.III	0.90	2.II with 2.III	0.86
1.II with 1.IV	0.96	2.II with 2.IV	0.95
1.II with 1.V	0.98	2.II with 2.V	0.98
1.III with 1.IV	0.91	2.III with 2.IV	0.86
1.III with 1.V	0.92	2.III with 2.V	0.88
1.IV with 1.V	0.99	2.IV with 2.V	0.98

Sources: Table estimated by Mr. James Trask. Data from tables 2-1, 2-2, 3-5, 3-8, 4-2, 4-3, and 5-1.

[a]The notation is set forth in table 6-3.

state its maximum and minimum net benefits. The two figures are subsequently added algebraically to the original per-capita income of the state, and its two new ranks are compared with the old one. The results of this calculation are shown in table 6-7.

It is now possible to establish certain conclusions with regard to the relative position of each state before and after the introduction of the federal government. These are summarized in table 6-8.

As table 6-8 indicates, the position of eighteen states has unambiguously improved. The position of twenty states has unambiguously deteriorated. For eleven states the result is indeterminate, because they have both gained and lost depending on the particular incidence assumption. Finally, the position of New York was unaffected: it retained the second place both before and after the introduction of the federal budget.

This interpretation of net fiscal incidence confirms our earlier conclusion about the regional impacts of federal fiscal policy. Although there are some exceptions, the general tenor appears to be a positive redistribution of income from the states along the East Coast and in the Midwest to the states in the West North Central and the Mountain regions.

Ranks afford a broad basis for general comparisons, but their usefulness is limited by the difficulty in assessing the importance of alternative rankings if

Table 6-7
Ranking of States According to Original Per-Capita Income and to Income under the Most and Least Favorable Incidence Assumptions
(rank order, from highest to lowest)

States	Original Income	Income under Most Favorable Assumption	Income under Least Favorable Assumption
Alabama	48	48	47
Alaska	5	1	1
Arizona	28	29	24
Arkansas	49	45	44
California	9	3	3
Colorado	13	18	13
Connecticut	1	5	6
Delaware	4	11	11
Florida	19	25	23
Georgia	33	43	43
Hawaii	8	4	4
Idaho	36	33	33
Illinois	6	6	5
Indiana	20	31	31
Iowa	23	19	27
Kansas	18	12	16
Kentucky	43	44	42
Louisiana	46	46	45
Maine	42	39	38
Maryland	10	15	15
Massachusetts	12	10	8
Michigan	11	13	12
Minnesota	24-25	23	19
Mississippi	50	50	49
Missouri	26	27	21
Montana	31	14	20
Nebraska	21	17	28
Nevada	7	9	9
New Hampshire	30	37	35
New Jersey	3	8	7
New Mexico	45	34	36
New York	2	2	2
North Carolina	34	47	48
North Dakota	37	20	41
Ohio	14	26	25
Oklahoma	35	38	32

Table 6-7 (cont.)

States	Original Income	Income under Most Favorable Assumption	Income under Least Favorable Assumption
Oregon	27	28	22
Pennsylvania	17	24	18
Rhode Island	15	16	14
South Carolina	47	49	50
South Dakota	39	21	29
Tennessee	41	42	46
Texas	32	40	40
Utah	38	41	37
Vermont	40	36	39
Virginia	24-25	32	30
Washington	16	22	17
West Virginia	44	35	34
Wisconsin	29	30	26
Wyoming	22	7	10

Sources: Table compiled by the author. Data from table 6-3 and the *Survey of Current Business* (U.S. Department of Commerce, Bureau of Economic Analysis, various issues).
Note: The District of Columbia has been omitted from this table. See p. 93, n. a.

different criteria are applied. States vary in their economic, social, and demographic characteristics; therefore, the *same* ranking may be given a *different* interpretation depending on the particular feature that underlies the comparison.

An essential aspect of net fiscal incidence involves the per-capita distribution of income *as a whole*. One may thus pose the following question: how has the overall distribution of income been affected by the introduction of the federal budget? Has it become more or less even than before? This question is resolved by calculating a measure of variability—the standard deviation—of the original distribution of income and comparing it with the dispersion of the distributions associated with each of the ten patterns of net fiscal incidence that have been obtained. The statistics are as summarized in table 6-9.

The results of table 6-9 indicate that the spatial activity of the federal government contributes to a more uniform income distribution across the states. The second variant of public goods ("public goods enter directly the utility of individuals") yields a more even distribution than the first variant ("public goods are intermediate inputs in the production of federal private goods"). This result confirms the conclusion based on the analysis of table 6-6. Not surprisingly, the most "equitable" distribution obtains when the former interpretation of public goods is combined with the hypothesis that the burden of the corporate profits tax falls on owners of corporate capital (assumption 2.II).

Table 6-8
Relative Positions of States After Introduction of Federal Budget

Per-Capita Income Rank			
Improved	*Deteriorated*	*Indeterminate*	*Unchanged*
Alabama	Colorado	Arizona	New York
Alaska	Connecticut	Iowa	
Arkansas	Delaware	Kentucky	
California	Florida	Missouri	
Hawaii	Georgia	Nebraska	
Idaho	Illinois	North Dakota	
Kansas	Indiana	Oklahoma	
Louisiana	Maryland	Oregon	
Maine	Michigan	Rhode Island	
Massachusetts	Nevada	Utah	
Minnesota	New Hampshire	Wisconsin	
Mississippi	New Jersey		
Montana	North Carolina		
New Mexico	Ohio		
South Dakota	Pennsylvania		
Vermont	South Carolina		
West Virginia	Tennessee		
Wyoming	Texas		
	Virginia		
	Washington		

Source: Based on table 6-7.
Note: The District of Columbia has been omitted from this table. See p. 93, n.a.

Federal Spatial Activity: How Close to
Explicit Redistributive Instruments?

It was argued in chapter 1 that some understanding of the distribution of public sector activity in the spatial dimension is central to an evaluation of particular tax and expenditure patterns of government, even in the absence of explicit regional redistribution policies. The question arises, therefore, to what degree can the spatial activity of the federal government be interpreted as a complement to other redistributive public programs?

To answer such a question it is necessary to compare net benefits with a benchmark that, at least in principle, represents a conscious policy of redistribution. A reasonable yardstick is provided by the revenue sharing program of the federal government, which allots federal money to jurisdictions that meet certain objective criteria. The amount of money distributed to each state is determined by two revenue-sharing formulas: each state is allotted a grant equal to the larger of the amounts due it under the distribution formula first passed by the Senate and the one initially approved by the House of Representatives.

The comparison between the findings of this study and the impact of revenue sharing on the states was based on the position of each state relative to the U.S. average under the two frameworks. Robert Reischauer has calculated the per-capita distribution of revenue-sharing money across states and the District of Columbia relative to the national average.[1] An analogous index was calculated for the ten alternative estimates of net fiscal incidence obtained in this study. The *Spearman* correlation between the revenue-sharing index for each state and its index under the ten patterns of fiscal incidence was subsequently calculated. The results are summarized in table 6-10.

The correlations between per-capita revenue-sharing allotments and per-capita net benefits are moderate, but they point in the right direction. That rank correlations are imperfect does not necessarily imply that the tax and expenditure policies of the central government are wanting in redistributive potential. On the contrary, it may well be the case that the political compromise of using two revenue-sharing formulas has considerably affected the neutrality of that program.

To check the findings of this study against a measure of need *par excellence,* we sought to discover the direction and degree of association between net benefits and the number of households below poverty level in each state. The results of this calculation are summarized in table 6-11. Both the direction and the degree of the rank correlations indicate a significant positive relationship between the fiscal activity of the federal government and the official measure of poverty in this country. The values of the coefficients, which turned out to be higher than those between net benefits and revenue sharing, should be assessed in the light of some very low correlations that Reischauer reports between per-capita revenue-sharing allotments and other measures of need.[2]

In conclusion, the activity of the federal government, aside from its other pursuits and objectives, may also be reasonably regarded as a complement to conscious regional redistribution policies of the Congress.

A Résumé of Difficulties and Reservations

It is difficult to avoid reiterating at this juncture that referring to taxes and expenditures expressed in dollar amounts as, respectively, "burdens" and "benefits" is at best an optimistic attitude. Of course every possible effort was made to take into account the results of economic theory regarding shifting and incidence (with much less success on the expenditure than on the tax side). But

Table 6-9
Dispersion of Alternative Income Distributions

(in dollars per person)

	Mean	Standard Deviation
Original Income Distribution, 1972	$4,255	$588
Income Distribution Under Incidence:[a]		
1.I	$4,480	$494
1.II	4,500	478
1.III	4,463	490
1.IV	4,513	498
1.V	4,500	487
2.I	4,459	453
2.II	4,472	429
2.III	4,443	455
2.IV	4,488	456
2.V	4,481	443

Sources: Table estimated by the author. Data from table 6-3 and the *Survey of Current Business* (U.S. Department of Commerce, Bureau of Economic Analysis, various issues).
[a]The notation is set forth in table 6-3.

Table 6-10
Spearman Rank Correlation Coefficients between Revenue Sharing and Alternative Net Benefit Allocations

Per-Capita Revenue Sharing with Net Fiscal Incidence:[a]	Correlation Coefficient
1.I	0.53
1.II	0.51
1.III	0.53
1.IV	0.52
1.V	0.52
2.I	0.54
2.II	0.51
2.III	0.51
2.IV	0.52
2.V	0.52

Sources: Table estimated by Mr. James Trask. Data from tables 2-1, 2-2, 3-5, 3-8, 4-2, 4-3, 5-1, and Reischauer, "General Revenue Sharing," table 2.
[a]The notation is set forth in table 6-3.

the fact remains that this analysis reflects income-equivalent differentials rather than genuine differences in utility. Similarly, equating total burdens to total taxes and total benefits to total costs of federal programs is a necessary evil arising from the empirical inability to account for higher order effects that would result within a general-equilibrium framework.

As far as statistical difficulties are concerned, it is not believed that they have significantly altered the final results. Nevertheless, it would be worthwhile to reestimate some allocations if it becomes possible in the future to obtain direct data on an item for which a proxy statistical series was used in the present investigation. A case in point, for instance, would be to discover information on corporate payrolls for the allocation of the corporate profits tax under the assumption of "full backward shifting."

In a different dimension, empirical difficulties were encountered with some of the control totals, which were the direct consequence of a benchmark revision in the concepts of the *Survey of Current Business* in 1976. On balance, the net result of such complications—especially with regard to the expenditure side—was to use, wherever possible, direct distributions available from other sources. For example, grants-in-aid were obtained directly from the 1972 *Census of Governments,* and it is believed that the accuracy in the distribution *per se* more than compensates for the small discrepancy in the total figure between this document and the *Survey of Current Business.*

Table 6-11
Spearman **Rank Correlation Coefficients between Poverty Households and Alternative Net Benefit Allocations**

Percent of Households Below Poverty Level with Net Fiscal Incidence:[a]	Correlation Coefficient
1.I	0.59
1.II	0.64
1.III	0.64
1.IV	0.60
1.V	0.61
2.I	0.68
2.II	0.71
2.III	0.72
2.IV	0.69
2.V	0.71

Source: Table estimated by Mr. James Trask. Data from tables 2-1, 2-2, 3-5, 3-8, 4-2, 4-3, 5-1, and *The County and City Data Book* (U.S. Department of Commerce, Bureau of the Census, 1972).

[a]The notation is set forth in table 6-3.

As a final word of caution in the interpretation of net fiscal incidence (which is the culmination of this investigation), the reader is reminded that the results of this study represent the fiscal impacts of only the federal government. Therefore, they do not necessarily delineate the pattern of net transfers that might arise if all levels of government were also taken into consideration.

Conclusion

The purpose of this study has been to examine, measure, and analyze the distribution of federal sector activity in the spatial dimension. Earlier in this chapter we analyzed the findings of the study and drew inferences about their implications. Compiling these individual results leads us to the following single most important conclusion: *the distribution of income is basically affected by expenditures and not by taxes.* There is a strong correlation between per-capita regional income and all assumptions of per-capita tax burden allocations:

Correlation of per-capita income with

Per-capita tax burden	I	0.93
Per-capita tax burden	II	0.92
Per-capita tax burden	III	0.88
Per-capita tax burden	IV	0.90
Per-capita tax burden	V	0.93

There can be little doubt that the regional impact of federal taxes may be adequately explained in terms of the per-capita distribution of personal income.

On the other hand, the variability of federal expenditures on private goods shows a weak correlation with income and an even weaker one with population. The coefficients are, respectively, 0.36 and 0.22. These are very rough summary statistics, but they do suggest that expenditures are influenced by noneconomic factors. They also explain why the pattern of net fiscal incidence is basically determined by the idiosyncracies of the private goods allocation.

While empirical regularities may be observed in public expenditures, they should not always be interpreted as being evidence that a particular pattern can be confirmed. The collective nature of public bodies makes it very difficult, if not impossible, to derive consistent estimates of expenditure patterns even under identical "objective circumstances." Different fiscal behavior may result from the collective nature of public decisions. For unlike taxation, which is levied in pecuniary terms upon well-defined bases (income, profits, wealth), public expenditures can be determined by such diverse factors as social conditions, demographic trends, and even sheer political compromises. Consequently, identification of general behavioral relationships proves a difficult and perhaps unstable process.

In conclusion, it is not easy to correlate federal outlays with a single economic or demographic indicator. Therefore, *the peculiarities of specific expenditure allocations have a major effect on the overall picture of fiscal incidence.* This observation implies that the results of incidence studies that deal exclusively with the tax side of the budget may be not only inadequate but also misleading.

There is little doubt that the accuracy of investigations such as ours will improve substantially as the uncertainty about the proper evaluation of burdens and benefits by the parties involved is gradually eliminated. At present, however, the conclusions are a reflection of income differentials rather than the outcome of genuine variations in consumer utility as perceived by the individuals themselves. But until such time as operational empirical results become available, this is the only feasible approach.

Notes

1. Robert D. Reischauer, "General Revenue Sharing—The Program's Incentives," ch. 3 in W. Oates (ed.), *Financing the New Federalism*, no. 5 in *The Governance of Metropolitan Regions*, Baltimore: Johns Hopkins Press, 1975.

2. Ibid., p. 49.

Appendixes

Appendices

Appendix A: Computational Details of the Sorting Procedure for Excise Taxes

The computer program ranks the processing industries of the U.S. Input-Output (I-O) structure according to the proportional participation of each taxed industry in their final "values."

The first computational step estimates the "matrix of values," namely a (362 × 8) matrix whose elements are the coefficient of total requirements of each taxed industry per unit of final demand of every processing industry multiplied by personal consumption expenditures on the processing industry. The 8 columns correspond to the taxed industries, whereas the 362 rows correspond to the total number of industries in the I-O structure. (Actually, the complete I-O table contains 367 elements, but 5 of them represent dummy industries, which are of no interest for the present purposes.) One industry, namely "chemical products," was sorted on the 85-industry classification of the 1967 I-O table. That industry was a net addition to the scheme in the case of customs duties and, in view of the reduction from a four-digit to a two-digit scheme (see appendix B), it was unnecessary to use the original extensive classification.

The second computational step normalizes, by columns, the elements of the previous matrix, so that the contributions are expressed as percentages; to put it differently, the sums of the eight columns are now equal to one.

The third step, which is the core of the program, ranks the processing industries of the I-O structure in accordance with the proportional participation of each taxed industry in their final "values." In the final matrix the diagonal elements are computed so as to reflect the proportion of the revenues to be allocated directly—that is, according to the personal consumption expenditures of the industry itself.

Graphic Representation of the Sorting Procedure

In figures A-1 to A-9, industries are listed along the abscissa, and the cumulative percentages of total "value" covered are listed along the ordinate. Therefore, a point on the graph represents the number of ranked industries (its x coordinate) required to achieve a given total percentage of coverage (its y coordinate). As mentioned in the text, virtually complete coverage is achieved before the total number of industries is exhausted.

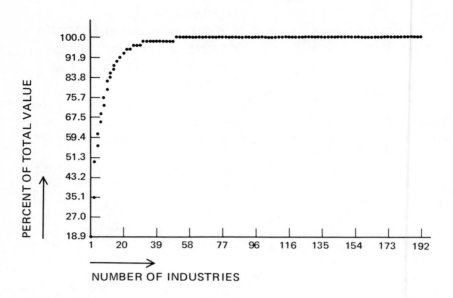

Figure A-1. Graphic Representation of Sorting Procedure for Sugar

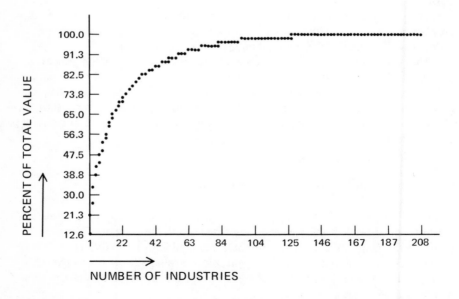

Figure A-2. Graphic Representation of Sorting Procedure for Petroleum

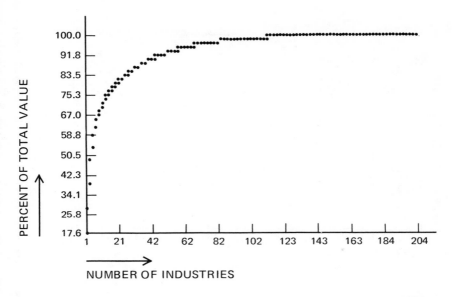

Figure A-3. Graphic Representation of Sorting Procedure for Tires and Tubes

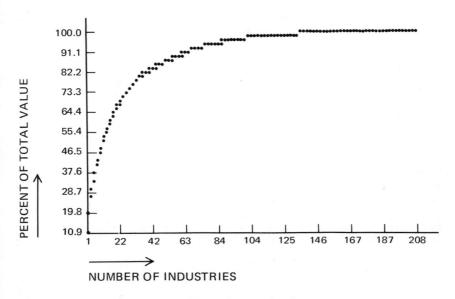

Figure A-4. Graphic Representation of Sorting Procedure for Rubber

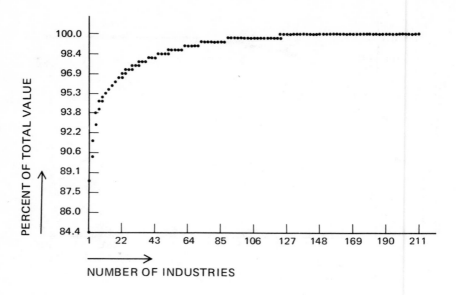

Figure A-5. Graphic Representation of Sorting Procedure for Trucks and Buses

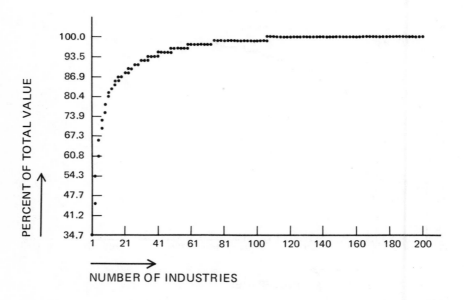

Figure A-6. Graphic Representation of Sorting Procedure for Truck Trailers

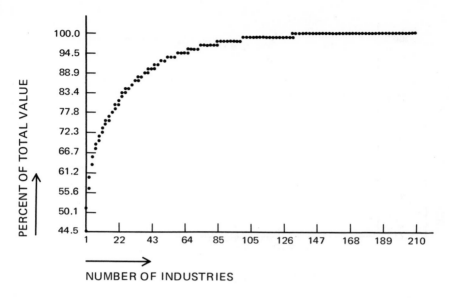

Figure A-7. Graphic Representation of Sorting Procedure for Motor Vehicles

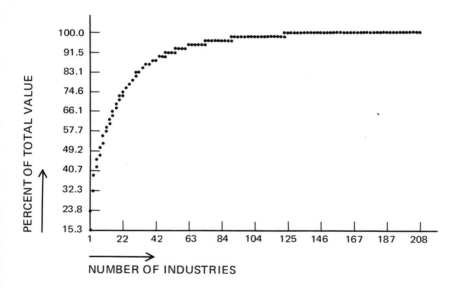

Figure A-8. Graphic Representation of Sorting Procedure for Communications

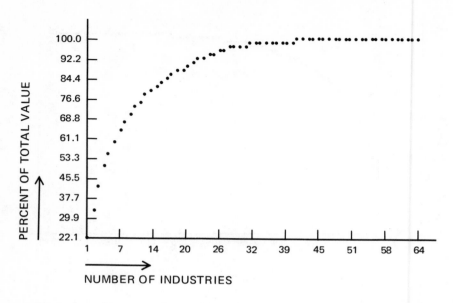

Figure A-9. Graphic Representation of Sorting Procedure for Chemicals

Appendix B:
Selection of Weights
for the Allocation of
Excise Taxes

Selective Sales Taxes

The first step was to establish the correspondence between the Input-Output (I-O) classification and the Standard Industrial Classification (SIC). The correspondence was achieved with the help of the *Standard Industrial Classification Manual*,[1] and it relates to the requisite number of weights for the coverage of a given percentage for every taxable industry. The results are summarized in table B-1.

As it becomes obvious from table B-1, there is an astonishing number of required weights for almost every industry, even for modest amounts of coverage. The number becomes prohibitive if it is realized that figures will have to be obtained for all fifty states. It is apparent that a reduction in the number of weights was in order at this juncture.

Such reduction was first completed by collapsing the four-digit classification to a two-digit one. A two-digit classification reflects "major industries" and has been used in past I-O studies. Although this regrouping was initiated for reasons of convenience, it was not theoretically unjustified; in fact, it contributed to the solution of certain conceptual problems that had arisen in connection with the I-O classification and the SIC discussed earlier. More specifically, at the four- or three-digit level of detail, the correspondence could not always be unambiguously identified, and neither the official sources nor our intuition could guide us in choosing the most appropriate items. For instance, I-O industry 14.18 ("bakery products") could in principle be allocated either by SIC 546 ("retail bakeries"), or by SIC 541 ("grocery stores"), or by SIC 5812 ("eating places"), or perhaps by a combination of these weights. Similarly, I-O industry 59.03 ("motor vehicles and parts") could in principle be allocated either by SIC 551 ("motor vehicle dealers"), or by a possible combination of SIC 551 and SIC 553 ("auto and home supply stores"). It was difficulties of this nature that were eliminated by compressing the extensive classification system to a general two-digit scheme.

But the major step toward the reduction of the total number of distributive weights was achieved by observing and taking advantage of the fact that, after the regrouping of weights under a two-digit classification, many taxable industries included several common elements. The problem, therefore, was to find the optimal intersection of weights—that is, the minimum number required for a desired level of coverage.

This problem was addressed by a series of successive approximations, which

115

were functions of (1) the relative importance of individual weights in each industry, (2) the relative frequency of weights, and (3) the availability of respective statistical series. In most cases these considerations were at conflict with each other, and a careful examination of the available trade-offs was taken into account.

Table B-1
Value of Taxable Industries Covered by Standard Industrial Classification (SIC) Weights

Taxable Industry	Cumulative Percentage Covered	Required Total Number of SIC Weights
Sugar	18	3
	79	9
	90	11
Petroleum	12	1
	50	23
	71	43
Tires, tubes	17	2
	52	15
	74	41
Rubber	11	2
	50	22
	71	41
Trucks, buses	84	2
	90	5
	93	11
Truck trailers	34	2
	59	7
	78	34
Motor vehicles	44	1
	62	15
	78	40
Communications	15	1
	44	13
	71	46

Sources: Table estimated and compiled by the author. Data from the *Input-Output Structure of the U.S. Economy*: 1967, vols. 1, 2, 3 (U.S. Department of Commerce, Office of Business Economics; published as a supplement to the *Survey of Current Business*); *Census of Retail Trade*, 1972 (U.S. Department of Commerce, Social and Economic Statistics Administration, Bureau of the Census); and the *Standard Industrial Classification Manual* (Office of Management and Budget, Executive Office of the President, 1972).

The final scheme to which this process converged includes twelve distributive weights. A discussion of its features is given in chapter 3 (p. 43).

Customs Duties

In the case of customs duties the selection of weights was more involved than in the case of selective sales taxes, because the great number of individual items presented us with several conflicting alternatives. Here, for example, the selected set would have to cover not only "intermediate" goods but also "final" commodities.

The first problem involved "miscellaneous manufactured articles" and "manufactured goods," both of which were classified in the "final goods" category. For the first group there were three alternatives:

1. Allocation by "total retail trade": this is a crude way, but the corresponding weight was already available from the allocation of excise taxes.

2. Allocation by "miscellaneous shopping goods stores" (SIC code 594): this method would improve the accuracy, but it required an additional weight.

3. Allocation partly by "miscellaneous shopping goods stores" and partly by "apparel and accessory stores": this alternative was based on the observation that clothing and footwear contribute over 60 percent to total value of duty for this group. Therefore, an even more accurate method would have been to use sales of apparel and accessory stores (SIC code 56) for the allocation of 60 percent of total duty, and sales of miscellaneous shopping goods stores (SIC code 594) for the remaining 40 percent. This method would have required again only one extra weight, namely 594, because the other one was already available. Therefore, the actual choice was between this method and the first one described here.

For the case of "manufactured goods"—a group that contains many disparate items—there were two alternatives:

1. Allocation by "total retail trade."

2. Allocation by "total retail trade" and by "apparel and accessory stores," in which case all components except textiles would be lumped together under the assumption that they are accurately reflected in total retail sales. The relative weights would then be the proportional participation of textiles (35 percent) and of the remaining items (65 percent) to the total value of collected duty.

A final choice was reserved until the category of "intermediate commodities" was also examined.

The selection of weights for imports used as inputs in other industries was based on the sorting program, a graphic representation of which was given in appendix A. The step-by-step methodology has been described in detail in appendix A and shall not be repeated here. The procedure reduces to selecting an "optimal" intersection of the three sets of weights sorted for the three "intermediate" imports.

There were three potential candidates:

Scheme I contained the following weights—(1) "retail trade," (2) "food stores," (3) "apparel and accessory stores," (4) "real estate," (5) "automotive dealers," (6) "insurance carriers," (7) "personal services," (8) "auto repair," (9) "amusement and recreation," (10) "medical and other health services," (11) "educational services," and (12) "nonprofit organizations."

Scheme II contained all of the weights in scheme I, plus "drug and propriety stores."

Scheme III contained all of the weights of scheme I, plus "miscellaneous shopping goods stores."

Table B-2 summarizes the coverage achieved by each of these schemes. In terms of their quantitative contributions, scheme 2 ranks first, scheme 3 second, and scheme 1 third. On the other hand, scheme 1 has the advantage of containing only weights that are already available from the distribution of excise taxes. Conversely, the other two schemes achieve a better coverage only upon the addition of an additional distributive series.

At this juncture the alternatives described earlier in connection with "imports for final consumption" were taken into account: it was pointed out above that SIC code 594 ("miscellaneous shopping goods stores") could contribute to a more accurate allocation of the most important group, namely "miscellaneous manufactured articles." It therefore became obvious that, on balance, scheme 3 is preferable to either scheme 1 or 2 because, apart from its acceptable quantitative coverage, it would also improve the accuracy of estimation in a very important area.

The final set of weights is given in chapter 3 (p. 48).

Table B-2
Value of Dutiable Industries Covered by Weights of Three Alternative Schemes

Industries	Percentage of Value Covered		
	Scheme 1	Scheme 2	Scheme 3
Chemicals and selected chemical products	60	71	62
Motor vehicles and parts	73	73	73
Petroleum refining and related products	55	56	55

Sources: Table estimated and compiled by the author. Data from the *Input-Output Structure of the U.S. Economy*: 1967, vols. 1, 2, 3 (U.S. Department of Commerce, Office of Business Economics; published as a supplement to the Survey of Current Business); *Census of Retail Trade*, 1972 (U.S. Department of Commerce, Social and Economic Statistics Administration, Bureau of the Census); *Highlights of the U.S. Export and Import Trade* (U.S. Department of Commerce, Bureau of the Census, Report FT990, Table I3); and the *Standard Industrial Classification Manual* (Office of Management and Budget, Executive Office of the President, 1972).

Note

1. *Standard Industrial Classification Manual,* Office of Management and Budget, Executive Office of the President 1972.

Appendix C: Theoretical Results of the Aaron-McGuire Model

Granted its restrictive assumption of an additively separable utility function, the Aaron-McGuire model provides a general framework for deriving allocation formulas based on the elasticity of marginal utility of income. To show this more clearly, consider the general form of the marginal utility:

$$MU_i(Y) = A Y_i^\theta \tag{C.1}$$

where $MU_i(Y)$ is marginal utility of income and Y_i is private income of individual i, θ is the elasticity of marginal utility, and A is an arbitrary constant. We shall next derive three allocation formulas associated with three different values of θ.

Case 1: Elasticity of Marginal Utility = 0. If $\theta = 0$, then equation (C.1) yields

$$MU_i(Y) = A \tag{C.2}$$

In turn, equation (C.2) implies a linear utility function:

$$U_i = A Y_i + C \tag{C.3}$$

where C is arbitrary.

The allocation rule implied by equation (C.3) may be obtained as follows: As shown in the text,

$$YP_i = \frac{k}{MU_i(Y)} \times P \tag{C.4}$$

where YP_i is the value of public goods to individual i, P is the value of total public goods available, and k is a constant. But it is also true that

$$\sum_i YP_i = P \tag{C.5}$$

Using equation (C.5) in connection with equation (C.4) we get

$$YP_i = \frac{P}{MU_i(Y) \sum_i \dfrac{1}{MU_i(Y)}} \tag{C.6}$$

In the case at hand $MU_i(Y) = A.$ Substituting this value into equation (C.6) we finally arrive at:

$$YP_i = \frac{P}{N} \qquad \text{(C.7)}$$

where N is the number of individuals. Equation (C.7) therefore reflects the well-known rule of "per-capita" allocation of benefits, which is seen to result from the assumption of zero elasticity of marginal utility of income.

Case 2: Elasticity of Marginal Utility = −1. If $\theta = -1$, equation (C.1) yields

$$MU_i(Y) = A Y_i^{-1} \qquad \text{(C.8)}$$

Equation (C.8) in turn implies that the corresponding utility function is of the form

$$U_i = A \ln Y_i + C \qquad \text{(C.9)}$$

where A and C are arbitrary constants.

The allocation rule implied by equation (C.9) is derived by substituting equation (C.8) into equation (C.6):

$$YP_i = \frac{Y_i}{\sum\limits_i Y_i} \times P \qquad \text{(C.10)}$$

Equation (C.10) thus reflects the well-known valuation procedure in proportion to income. The main implication is that the incidence of benefits follows a proportional pattern.

Case 3: Elasticity of Marginal Utility = −2. If $\theta = -2$, equation (C.1) yields

$$MU_i(Y) = A Y_i^{-2} \qquad \text{(C.11)}$$

Equation (C.11) in turn implies that the underlying utility function is of the form

$$U_i = E - \frac{C}{Y_i} \qquad \text{(C.12)}$$

where E and C are arbitrary constants. The corresponding allocation rule is derived by substituting equation (C.11) back into equation (C.6):

$$YP_i = \frac{Y_i^2}{\sum\limits_i Y_i^2} \times P \tag{C.13}$$

The important conclusion embodied in equation (C.13) is that the incidence of benefits turns out to be "regressive," in the sense that the higher the income, the greater the amount of benefits received.

As is evident from these illustrations, the rule for the allocation of benefits depends crucially upon the rate at which marginal utility diminishes. This implies that the distribution of income, as far as the imputation of public goods is concerned, will depend on the value of the elasticity of marginal utility. To show this more clearly, let

Y_a = private income of individual a

YP_a = imputed "public good" income of individual a

Y_b = private income of individual b

YP_b = imputed "public good" income of individual b

Forming the ratio of the two incomes and differentiating with respect to public goods, we obtain

$$\frac{\partial}{\partial P}\left(\frac{Y_a + YP_a}{Y_b + YP_b}\right) = \frac{(k/A)Y_a Y_b (Y_a^{-(\theta+1)} - Y_b^{-(\theta+1)})}{((kP/A)Y_b^{-\theta} + Y_b)^2} \tag{C.14}$$

We distinguish again three cases:

$\theta = 0$. Equation (C.14) then reduces to

$$\frac{\partial}{\partial P}\left(\frac{Y_a + YP_a}{Y_b + YP_b}\right) = \frac{(k/A)Y_a Y_b (Y_a^{-1} - Y_b^{-1})}{((kP/A) + Y_b)^2} \tag{C.15}$$

Suppose that originally $Y_a > Y_b$. Then equation (C.15) yields:

$$\frac{\partial}{\partial P}\left(\frac{Y_a + YP_a}{Y_b + YP_b}\right) < 0$$

This means that after an increase in the amount of public goods the distribution of income has changed in favor of the poorer person. The explanation follows from the fact that with $\theta = 0$ the absolute amount of apportioned benefits is the same for all [see equation C.7)] ; hence, in relative terms it favors people with lower incomes.

$\theta = -1$. In this case, equation (C.14) vanishes. Thus

$$\frac{\partial}{\partial P}\left(\frac{Y_a + YP_a}{Y_b + YP_b}\right) = 0 \qquad (C.16)$$

Here the original distribution of income is not affected by the introduction of public goods because the allocation rule implied by $\theta = -1$ entails imputation of benefits proportional to income.

$\theta = -2$. Equation (C.14) now becomes

$$\frac{\partial}{\partial P}\left(\frac{Y_a + YP_a}{Y_b + YP_b}\right) = \frac{(k/A)Y_a Y_b(Y_a - Y_b)}{((kP/A)Y_b^2 + Y_b)^2} \qquad (C.17)$$

Suppose again, that $Y_a > Y_b$. Then, equation (C.17) implies that

$$\frac{\partial}{\partial P}\left(\frac{Y_a + YP_a}{Y_b + YP_b}\right) > 0$$

This means that an increase in the provision of public goods will result in a deterioration of income distribution as more benefits are distributed to higher income than to lower income people [see equation (C.13)]. In general, this is going to be the case so long as $|\theta| > 1$.

Bibliography

Aaron, H. and M. McGuire. "Efficiency and Equity in the Optimal Supply of a Public Good," *Review of Economics and Statistics* 51 (February 1969).

――――. "Public Goods and Income Distribution," *Econometrica* 38 (November 1970).

Adler, J.H. "The Fiscal System, the Distribution of Income, and Public Welfare," ch. III in Kenyon E. Poole, *Fiscal Policies and the American Economy*. Englewood Cliffs, N.J.: Prentice-Hall, 1951.

Annual Report of the Administration of Veterans Affairs, 1973.

Baumol, W. *Economic Theory and Operations Analysis,* 4th ed., Englewood Cliffs, N.J.: Prentice-Hall, 1976.

Break, G.F. "The Incidence and Economic Effects of Taxation," in A.S. Blinder, R.M. Solow, et al., *The Economics of Public Finance.* Studies of Government Finance. Washington, D.C.: The Brookings Institution, 1974.

Break, G.F., and J.A. Pechman. *Federal Tax Reform.* Studies of Government Finance. Washington, D.C.: The Brookings Institution, 1975.

Brennan, G. "The Distributional Implications of Public Goods," *Econometrica* 44 (March 1976).

Brittain, J.A. *The Payroll Tax for Social Security.* Studies of Government Finance. Washington, D.C.: The Brookings Institution, 1972.

Burkhead, J. and J. Miner. *Public Expenditure.* Chicago: Aldine Publishing Co., 1971.

Civil Aeronautics Board, *Commuter Air Carrier Traffic Studies, Year Ended 1972.*

Cragg, J.C., A.C. Harberger, and P. Mieszkowski. "Empirical Evidence on the Incidence of the Corporation Income Tax," *Journal of Political Economy* 75 (December 1967).

Distilled Spirits Institute, *Annual Statistical Review* (1972).

Dodge, D.A. "Impact of Tax, Retransfer, and Expenditure Policies of Government on the Distribution of Personal Income in Canada," *Review of Income and Wealth* 21 (March 1975).

Dusansky, R. "The Short-Run Shifting of the Corporation Income Tax in the United States," *Oxford Economic Papers* (November 1972).

Executive Office of the President, Office of Management and Budget, *Standard Industrial Classification Manual,* 1972.

Feldstein, M.S. and J. Brittain. "The Incidence of the Social Security Tax: Comment and Reply," *American Economic Review* 62 (September 1972).

Gillespie, I.W. *The Incidence of Taxes and Public Expenditures in the Canadian Economy,* no. 2 in Studies of the Royal Commission on Taxation, September 1964.

――――. "The Effects of Public Expenditures on the Distribution of Income:

An Empirical Investigation," in *Essays in Fiscal Federalism,* R. Musgrave, ed. Washington, D.C.: The Brookings Institution, 1976.

Gordon, R.J. "The Incidence of the Corporation Income Tax in U.S. Manufacturing," *American Economic Review* 54 (September 1967).

Hall, C.A., Jr. "Direct Shifting of the Corporation Income Tax in Manufacturing," *American Economic Review* 70 (May 1964).

Harberger, A.C., "The Incidence of the Corporation Income Tax," *Journal of Political Economy* 70 (June 1962).

Houthakker, H.S. and L.D. Taylor. *Consumer Demand in the United States: Analyses and Projections*, (2nd and enlarged ed.) Cambridge, Mass.: Harvard University Press, 1970.

Kosters, Marvin. "Effects of an Income Tax on Labor Supply," in A. Harberger and M. Baily, eds. *The Taxation of Income from Capital.* Washington, D.C.: The Brookings Institution, 1969.

Krzyzaniak, M. and R. Musgrave. *The Shifting of the Corporation Income Tax.* Baltimore: Johns Hopkins, 1963.

Lewellen, W.G. "An Intersectoral Analysis of Senior Executive Rewards," *Proceedings of the National Tax Association* (October 1969).

Maital, S. "Public Goods and Income Distribution: Some Further Results," *Econometrica* 41 (May 1973).

————. "Apportionment of Public Goods Benefits to Individuals," *Public Finance/Finances Publiques* no. 3 (1975).

Musgrave, R.A. *The Theory of Public Finance.* New York: McGraw-Hill, 1959.

Musgrave, R.A., J.J. Carroll, L.D. Cook, and L. Frane. "Distribution of Tax Payments by Income Groups: A Case Study for 1948," *National Tax Journal* 4, no. 1 (March 1951).

Musgrave, R.A., K.E. Case, and H.B. Leonard. "The Distribution of Fiscal Burdens and Benefits," *Public Finance Quarterly* 2 (July 1974).

Musgrave, R.A. and P.B. Musgrave. *Public Finance in Theory and Practice*, 2nd. ed. New York: McGraw-Hill, 1976.

Mushkin, S. "Distribution of Federal Taxes Among the States," *National Tax Journal* 9, no. 2 (June 1956).

————. "Distribution of Federal Expenditures Among the States," *The Review of Economics and Statistics* 39 (November 1957).

National Tobacco Tax Association, *Comparative Cigarette Tax Collections,* 1972.

Newcomer, M. *Studies in Current Tax Problems.* New York: Twentieth Century Fund, 1937.

The New York Times, October 10, 1943.

Nordhaus, W. and J. Tobin. "Is Growth Obsolete?" in *Economic Growth,* Fiftieth Anniversary Colloquium V. New York: National Bureau of Economic Research, 1972.

Pechman, J.A. *Federal Tax Policy*, 3rd ed. Studies of Government Finance. Washington, D.C.: The Brookings Institution, 1977.

Pechman, J.A. and B.A. Okner. *Who Bears the Tax Burden?* Studies of Government Finance. Washington, D.C.: The Brookings Institution, 1974.

Peskin, J. *In-kind Income and the Measurement of Poverty,* technical paper VII, U.S. Department of Health, Education, and Welfare. Washington, D.C.: 1976.

Reischauer, R. "General Revenue Sharing—The Program's Incentives," ch. 3 in W. Oates, ed. *Financing the New Federalism,* no. 5 in the Governance of Metropolitan Regions. Baltimore: Johns Hopkins, 1975.

Shoup, C. *Public Finance.* Chicago: Aldine Publishing Co., 1969.

_____. *Quantitative Research in Taxation and Government Expenditure,* Fiftieth Anniversary Colloquium IV. New York: National Bureau of Economic Research, 1972.

Shoven, J.B. and J. Whalley. "A General Equilibrium Calculation of the Effects of Differential Taxation of Income from Capital in the United States," *Journal of Public Economics* (November 1972).

Stockfisch, T.A. "On the Obsolescence of Incidence," *Public Finance/Finances Publiques* XIV (1959).

Tarasov, H. *Who Pays the Taxes?* Temporary National Economic Committee. Monograph no. 3, Washington, D.C.: U.S. Government Printing Office, 1941.

Tax Foundation, *Allocating the Federal Tax Burden by State.* Research aid no. 3 (revised). New York: 1964.

_____, *Federal Tax Burdens in States and Metropolitan Areas.* Research aid no. 5. New York: 1974.

Turek, J. "Short-Run Shifting of the Corporate Income Tax in Manufacturing, 1935-1965," *Yale Economic Essays* (Spring 1970).

U.S. Congress, House of Representatives, Intergovernmental Relations Subcommittee on Government Operations. *Federal Revenue and Expenditure Estimates for States and Regions, Fiscal Years 1965-1967,* 90th Congress, Second Session. Washington, D.C.: U.S. Government Printing Office, October 1968.

U.S. Department, of Commerce. *Statistical Abstract of the United States,* various years.

U.S. Department of Commerce, Bureau of the Census. *1972 Census of Governments.*

U.S. Department of Commerce, Bureau of the Census. *1972 Census of Retail Trade.*

U.S. Department of Commerce, Bureau of the Census. *County Business Patterns,* various years.

U.S. Department of Commerce, Bureau of the Census. *1972 County and City Data Book.*

U.S. Department of Commerce, Bureau of the Census. *Highlights of the U.S. Export and Import Trade.* Report FT990, 1972.

U.S. Department of Commerce, Bureau of Economic Analysis, Office of

Business Economics. *Definitions and Conventions of the 1967 Input-Output Study,* October 1974.

U.S. Department of Commerce, Bureau of Economic Analysis, Office of Business Economics. *Input-Output Structure of the U.S. Economy: 1967,* vol. 1, 2, and 3. (Published as a supplement to the Survey of Current Business).

U.S. Department of Commerce, Bureau of Economic Analysis. Office of Business Economics. *Survey of Current Business,* various issues.

U.S. Department of Defense, Office of the Assistant Secretary (Comptroller), *Defense Personnel and Total Population in the United States* by State, 1974.

U.S. Department of Health, Education, and Welfare. *Hospitals: A County and Metropolitan Area Data Book,* 1972.

U.S. Department of Health, Education, and Welfare, National Center for Educational Statistics. *Digest of Educational Statistics,* 1973.

U.S. Department of Health, Education, and Welfare, National Center for Educational Statistics. *Residence and Migration of College Students,* 1970.

U.S. Department of Health, Education, and Welfare, Social Security Administration, Social Security Bulletin. *Annual Statistical Supplement,* 1972.

U.S. Department of the Interior, Bureau of Outdoor Recreation. *Selected Outdoor Recreation Statistics,* 1972.

U.S. Department of Transportation, Federal Highway Administration. *Highway Statistics,* 1972.

U.S. Department of the Treasury, Internal Revenue Service. *Statistics of Income: Individual Income Tax Returns,* various years.

U.S. Department of the Treasury, Internal Revenue Service. *Statistics of Income: Fiduciary, Gift, and Estate Tax Returns,* various years.

U.S. Department of the Treasury, Internal Revenue Service. *Annual Report of the Commissioner of Internal Revenue,* 1972 and 1973.

Name Index

Aaron, H., 79, 81-82, 85, 87n, 121
Adler, J.H., 5

Baily, M.J., 16n
Baumol, W.J., 21, 32n
Blinder, A.S., 14n
Break, G.F., 10, 32n, 33n, 38, 53n
Brennan, G., 77, 87n
Brittain, J.A., 20, 32n
Burkhead, J., 58, 74n

Carroll, J.J., 13n
Case, K.E., 14n, 74n
Colm, G., 4, 13n
Cook, L.D., 13n
Cragg, J.G., 25-26, 33n

Dodge, D.A., 5, 10, 14n
Dusansky, R., 26, 33n

Feldstein, M.S., 32n
Frane, L., 13n
Friedman, M., 19

Gillespie, I.W., 5, 14n
Gordon, R.J., 25, 33n

Hall, C.A., Jr., 25-26, 33n
Harberger, A.C., 16n, 25-26, 33n
Houthakker, H.S., 38, 53n

Kosters, M., 16n, 32n
Krzyzaniak, M., 24-26, 33n

Leonard, H.B., 14n, 74n
Lewellen, W.G., 32n
Lindahl, E., 84

McGuire, M.C. 79, 81-82, 85, 87n, 121
Maital, S., 84-85, 87n
Mieszkowski, P., 25-26, 33n
Miner, J., 58, 74n
Musgrave, P.B., 14n, 32n
Musgrave, R.A., 4-5, 10, 13n, 14n, 24-26, 32n, 33n, 74n
Mushkin, S., 6-8, 14n, 60n

Newcomer, M., 4
Nordhaus, W.D., 76-77, 87n

Oates, W.E., 106n
Okner, B.A., 5, 14n

Pechman, J.A., 5, 14, 38, 53n
Peskin, J., 58, 74n
Poole, K.E., 14n

Reischauer, R., 102-103, 106n

Samuelson, P.A., 78
Scarf, H., 26
Shoup, C.S., 4, 13n, 59, 74n
Shoven, J.B., 26, 33n
Solow, R.M., 14n
Stockfisch, T.A., 9-10, 14n

Tarasov, H., 4, 13n
Taylor, L.D., 38, 53n
Tobin, J., 76-77, 87n
Tucker, R., 4
Turek, J., 26, 33n

Voorhees, E.M., 33n

Walk, H., 4
Whalley, J., 26, 33n
Wright, C., 16n

Subject Index

References to tables are printed in boldface type.

About the Author

Thanos Catsambas is currently assistant professor in the Department of Economics, Boston University. He was formerly a research associate at the Institution for Social and Policy Studies, Yale University. His main interests are public finance and the application of adaptive control techniques to econometrics. Dr. Catsambas is a summa cum laude, Phi Beta Kappa graduate of Yale College. He also holds the M.A., M.Phil., and Ph.D. degrees from Yale University.